Wetlands & Waterways

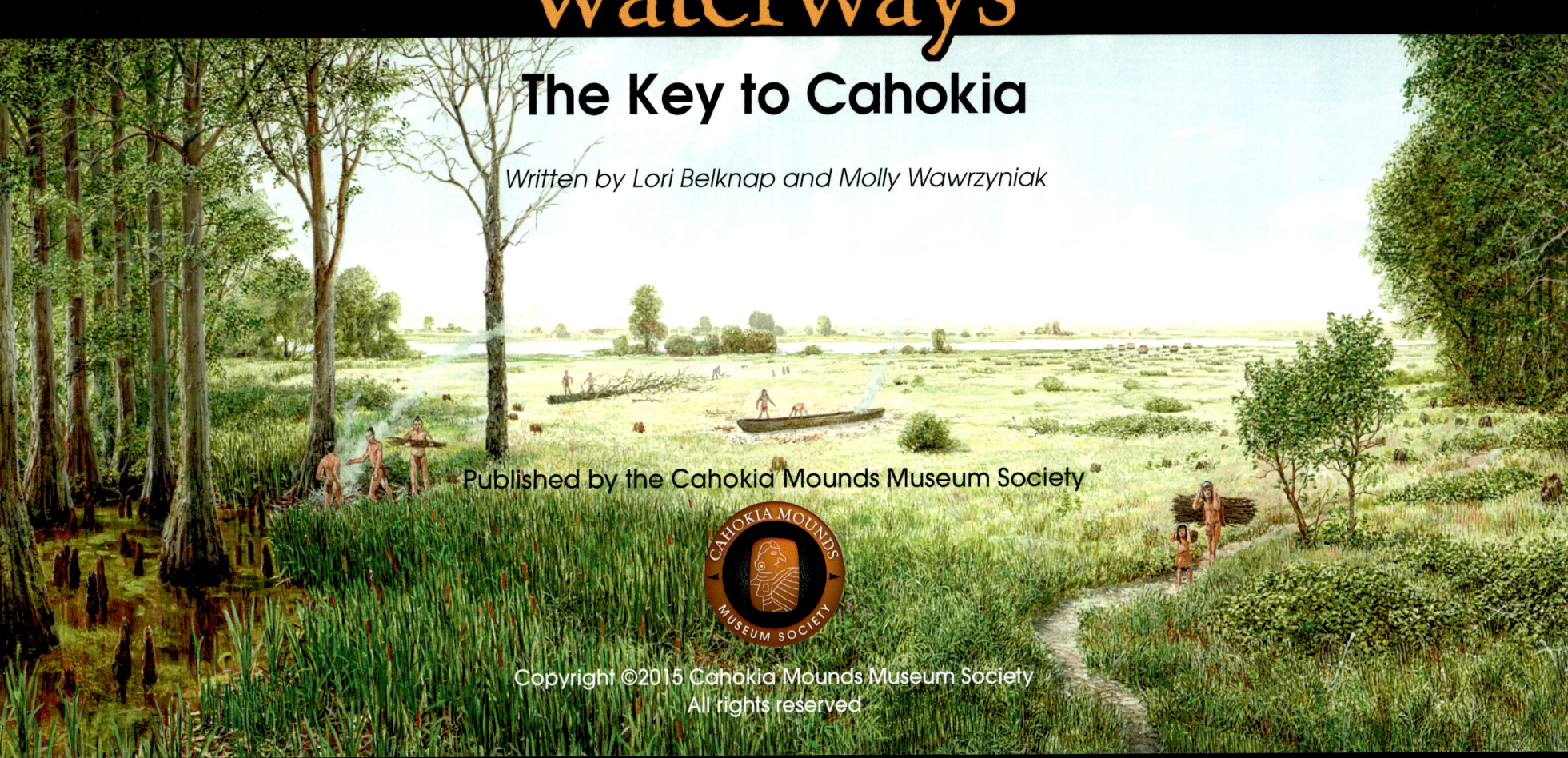

The Key to Cahokia

Written by Lori Belknap and Molly Wawrzyniak

Published by the Cahokia Mounds Museum Society

Copyright ©2015 Cahokia Mounds Museum Society
All rights reserved

ACKNOWLEDGEMENTS

There are many people in various capacities that have contributed to the production of this book, both directly and indirectly. The list would be too consuming to include everyone who has supported the authors in the production of this book. The following individuals deserve special acknowledgement for their contribution, in no particular order: The Cahokia Mounds Museum Society Board of Directors, Bill Iseminger, Mark Esarey, Ph.D., Jack Kerber, Ken Williams, Linda Krieg, John Kelly Ph.D., Jeffrey M. Mitchem Ph.D., Gayle Fritz Ph.D., Gene Stratmann, Matt Migalla, Gary Harmon, Rick Riccio, Jan Vriesen, Henri D. Grissino-Mayer Ph.D., Amy Creasy-Clark, Jay Rounds, Maris Boyd Gillette Ph.D., Lucretia Kelly Ph.D., Adam Celuch and INLANDESIGN, Heather Welch-Westfall, Taylor Studios, Inc., Rantoul, IL., The Great Pumpkin Patch, Arthur, IL., Cahokia Mounds Preservation Fund, Osage Nation, Herb Roe, Charles Pratt, Illinois State Archaeological Society, Steven L. Boles, James R. Duncan, and Ben Pollard.

Wetlands & Waterways: The Key to Cahokia
Copyright © 2015 by Cohokia Mounds Museum Society

ISBN 978-1-940244-41-9

All rights reserved. Except for brief excerpts for review purposes,
no part of this book may be reproduced or used in any form without
written permission from the publisher.

All images are property of and on file at Cahokia Mounds State Historic Site, unless otherwise credited in text.

Printed in the United States of America
by Custom Museum Publishing, Rockland, Maine

TABLE OF CONTENTS

Introduction 3

Grand Cahokia 5

An Amazing Discovery 33

An Aquatic Tradition 43

Connected Waterways 57

American Bottom Resources 69

Exhibit *Wetlands and Waterways: The Key to Cahokia* 83

Conclusion 94

Bibliography 96

View of Monks Mound, looking west with St. Louis on the horizon. Photo Courtesy, Matt Gush

INTRODUCTION

When Molly and I first discussed writing this book, our initial thoughts were to provide a "coffee table" accompaniment to the new *Wetlands and Waterway: The Key to Cahokia* exhibit. As we delved into the project, we thought about what story we wanted to tell and how best to portray the exhibit, and realized that a unique opportunity was at bay. An opportunity to not only fill a void in the body of literature that exists for our general visitors, but also to tell a unique story of Cahokia Mounds, and the people who lived here, within the framework of the ecology and landscape of the American Bottom. The goal of this book is to give an interpretation of the ancient canoe, which was donated to the site in 2009 and now on display in the gallery, give a description of the new exhibit, describe in some detail the resources available in the region, and to give a general summary of the Mississippian culture group that lived here about 1,000 years ago, who we call Cahokians.

Due to the significance and scope of this ancient archaeological site, referred to as Cahokia Mounds from this point forward, there is an abundance of literature regarding the site and the Cahokians who lived here. Publications range from highly-technical site reports to fictional novels. There are publications that focus on various aspects of the site including: the population, material culture, ideology, landscape modification, and technology, just to name a few. There are also different perspectives and interpretations about the site written by academics, archaeologists, and other interested parties. What we seek to do with this publication is to give our general visitor an overview of these topics, and how they relate to the new exhibit. We will summarize the resources that were available at that time, explain how the Mississippians utilized them, the role that dugout canoes played in the florescence of the city, and the general life-ways of the ancient culture.

Since 2009, when the canoe was donated to Cahokia Mounds State Historic Site (CMSHS), the site has planned to develop an exhibit to showcase the canoe and its role in Cahokia Mounds' history. In 2013, Molly Wawrzyniak, a graduate student in the museum studies program at the University of Missouri, St. Louis, MO joined the staff as a Graduate Research Assistant in an intensive two-year program. Molly was assigned to serve as the Project Coordinator for the *Wetlands and Waterways: The Key to Cahokia* exhibit, which was unveiled on August 15, 2015. The project was generously funded by the Cahokia Mounds Preservation Fund established by former Illinois State Treasurer, the late Judy Barr Topinka. This project was managed by the Cahokia Mounds Museum Society (CMMS), the not-for-profit support group of CMSHS. The administrators had several years to implement the project since the canoe required several years of conservation to ensure its integrity and suitability for display.

At its inception, the exhibit was a conceptual drawing by an exhibit designer currently working on another project at the site. In this concept, the ancient canoe served as the centerpiece of the exhibit. During the course of the project, the concept has gone from this initial drawing, to a 52-foot, content-rich exhibit, with a life-sized diorama, and separate exhibit display for the ancient canoe.

We hope that you enjoy this story-the story of Cahokia Mounds, a prehistoric city, built on a landscape teeming with resources and transportation routes, rich in material culture and ideology, by excellent farmers, craftsmen, and engineers. A place that dominated much of prehistoric Midwest and southeastern America for roughly 400 years, and whose cultural traits can still be found in various Native American groups today. A place that has been designated a World Heritage Site by the United Nations Educational, Scientific and Cultural Organization (UNESCO), a U.S. National Historic Landmark by the U.S. Dept. of Interior, National Park Service, a place revered by contemporary Native American people, and appreciated by millions of visitors. It is a place unique, spatially and temporally in North America, unparalleled in the minds of those who have been fortunate enough to experience its wonders, past and present.

—LORI BELKNAP
Executive Director, Cahokia Mounds Museum Society

Interpretive painting of the Grand Plaza looking north by L.K. Townsend.

GRAND CAHOKIA

About a thousand years ago a civilization arose in the fertile valley of the Mississippi, just outside of (and to a lesser degree including) what is now St. Louis. For roughly 400 years, a complex and dynamic city existed as one with the varied and rich environment that was integral to its development. Often referred to as civilization, city, state, or religious center, depending on who is doing the categorizing and what period is being described, the fact is rarely disputed that the site was a large, well-organized, sedentary settlement, and that it influenced the Midwest and southeastern United States during its time. Referred to as Cahokia Mounds, or simply "Cahokia," this community of about 10-20,000 during its zenith, was a hierarchical society that practiced large-scale agriculture, understood the scientific aspects of engineering, engaged in long-distance trade, and possessed a complex system of beliefs that was expressed in materials and objects of ceremony and status. Even though much has been learned from over 80 years of compiled research about the site, there is still much to be learned. Since they had no written language, we don't know how they referred to themselves or their city. They belonged to a cultural tradition that archaeologists call "Mississippian," which is found throughout the Mississippi Valley and the Southeast United States. We often refer to the people that lived at the site during its occupation as "Cahokians," even though the name actually derives from one of the sub-tribes of the Illiniwek (Illinois) Indians, the Cahokia, who moved into this area in the 1600s, long after the site had been abandoned by the Mississippians.

What we know about Cahokia comes from early historic accounts as well as early and on-going excavations at the site. Even though roughly only one percent of the site has been excavated, much has been learned about the physical aspects of their landscape as well as the intricacies of their culture and life-ways. The central portion of the archaeological site (2100 acres) is preserved and is now the Cahokia Mounds State Historic Site (CMSHS). CMSHS is located eight miles east of St. Louis in Collins-

ARCHAEOLOGY

ARCHAEOLOGY IS A SCIENTIFIC BRANCH OF THE ANTHROPOLOGY DISCIpline that studies and interprets human activity through the recovery and analysis of the material culture that has been left behind and the environmental and cultural impacts on and by them. When archaeologists work in the field they adhere to strict scientific methods and ethics set forth by professional and governmental institutions (such as the Society for American Archaeology and

Dr. James A. Brown and volunteers working at the Mound 34 site.

local and Federal laws regarding excavations). Since archaeology is a destructive science and the intact remains of human activity are destroyed by the scientific process of excavating, it is imperative that slow and controlled methods are used in the recovery and subsequent documentation of data. Field work involves the careful and meticulous task of removing soil to reveal the remains of human activity in the form of soil discolorations, artifacts, organic remains, and architecture. Maps, photographs, documentation, and soil descriptions are integral parts of the science of archaeology. Recovered objects and samples are then taken to a lab for processing where these items are cleaned, counted, measured, described, labeled, inventoried, and stored. Once these steps are completed, the analyses and interpretation of the data can then illuminate notions and test current hypotheses, often providing new theories to be tested. One of the important ethical standards adhered to by archaeologists is the timely dissemination and publishing of information resulting from investigations, generally the final stage in the process.

ville, Illinois. It is designated as a U.S. National Historic Landmark. In 1982 it was recognized by the United Nations Educational, Scientific, and Cultural Organization (UNESCO) as a World Heritage Site for its importance in the understanding of Native American prehistory and its importance to all mankind.

Prior to the rise of Cahokia there was a long history of pre-Columbian occupation in the region. Human history in the eastern woodlands is divided by archaeologists into several broad categories based on similarities such as house type, artifact style, settlement patterns, and subsistence methods. The cultural period parameters are not absolute, rather the divisions serve as a guideline to generally characterize one cultural tradition from another. The traditions generally accepted for the American Bottom region are PaleoIndian (9500-8000 BC), Archaic (8000-600 BC), Early Woodland (600-150 BC), Middle Woodland (150 BC-AD 300), Late Woodland (AD 300-750), Terminal Late Woodland/Emergent Mississippian (AD 750-1050), Mississippian (AD 1050-1350), Oneota (AD 1350-1600), Illinois Confederacy (AD

Reconstructed Emergent Mississippian pit-house.

Interpretive painting of market scene during Cahokia's peak by Michael Hampshire.

1600+) Historic Indian, Colonial, and American (AD 1673-Present) (Iseminger 2010). These periods are further divided into phases based on location/variations. Some of the characteristics of the Mississippian assemblage are evident in the Emergent Mississippian period that precedes it at Cahokia Mounds. During this transition, archaeologists have documented increasingly larger communities living in organized groups of houses situated around courtyard areas. At first, they lived in single-family homes, called pit-houses, having floors which were sunken about three feet into the ground. These so-called pit-houses were constructed using posts set into individual postholes to form the walls. Plant and animal resources abounded in the area but crop cultivation became more important, especially corn (maize), allowing for greater surpluses in crops and growth in population.

Population and complexity continued to grow and Cahokia Mounds reached its zenith as a community in the region at about AD 1100. This period is characterized by marked social differences and complex social organization, elaborate ritualism, ceramic items tempered with crushed mussel shell, large-scale agriculture, mound and plaza organization, craft specialization, extensive trade, and monumental architecture in the form of mounds and large wooden buildings. Houses were in shallower basins, or none at all, and instead of individual postholes, long narrow trenches were dug into which the wall posts were inserted. These are referred to as "wall-trench houses." At other Mississippian sites, most of these characteristics existed but at a smaller scale. Smaller multiple-mound

CERAMICS

CAHOKIAN POTTERY IS GENERALLY DESCRIBED AS SOME OF THE finest among pre-contact Native ceramics. Generally, it has thin and smooth walls, grey to cream or buff in color (excluding the slip), and tempered with crushed burned mussel shell. Sometimes pieces reflected their cosmological beliefs with elements representing animals or people, whether real or fantastic. Cahokian vessels range from practical objects like jars and bowls to more elaborate ceremonial objects such as engraved beakers or effigy vessels.

The process of shaping clay then firing it to yield a durable object was developed at different times and places throughout the world, but, generally speaking, this process was a relatively new technology compared to the production of other implements. Variations in forms and decorations are indicative of space and time, making the analyses of ceramics an important tool for archaeologists in the interpretation of archaeological remains. In this region, pottery first appears about 500-600 BC.

The raw materials for making ceramics generally include three basic ingredients: clay, a sticky sediment that becomes moldable when wet, inclusions of mineral or organic materials that either naturally exist or are added to the clay to make it more workable and to limit

continued ▶

Cahokian effigy vessel depicting a beaver.

Cahokian Ramey incised ceramic container.

Ceramics continued.

shrinkage, referred to as "temper," and water. Other things can be added, such as pigments, but are not necessarily required to produce a finished product. Tempers used by potters vary culturally. Some of the materials used by potters locally are grit (crushed rock or limestone), sand, grog (crushed pottery), and shell. The use of crushed riverine shell as a temper is a hallmark of Mississippian pottery, but some earlier pieces still contain grog and grit temper.

Mississippian potters used a "coiling" method for construction, where clay was rolled into long strips that were progressively stacked on top of each other to form the basic shape. Then the coils were smoothed out using a paddle, sometimes cord-wrapped, which left cord impressions in the vessel surface, or the coils were smoothed out by hand or a smooth paddle. Many Mississippian vessels were slipped with a pigmented clay wash, or decorated with incising or engraving.

Interpretive painting of Mississippian dwelling construction by Michael Hampshire.

Mississippian satellite communities have been documented in the area, as were single-mound communities, villages, and moundless hamlets, all of which were likely governed in some way by Cahokia. Mitchell, Illinois, for example, was a community consisting of 11 mounds located just seven miles north of Cahokia Mounds. Cahokia Mounds consisted of 120 mounds, East St. Louis had 45 mounds, and 26 mounds were documented in St. Louis. Today, archaeologists often refer to this complex as "Greater Cahokia."

Cahokians understood geometric principles necessary for

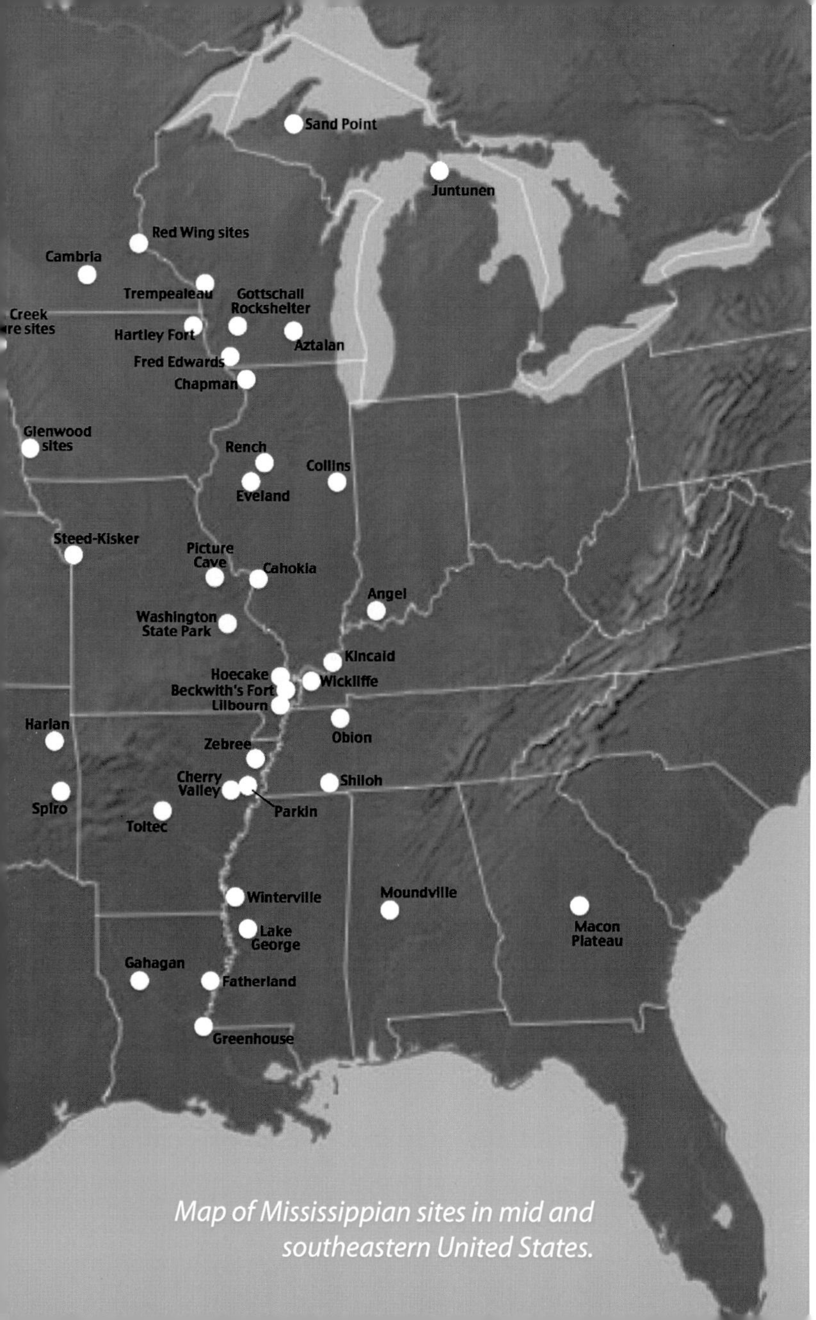

site planning and the resources to conduct large-scale public works projects such as the monumental architecture, still evident at the site in the 100-foot tall Monks Mound and the circa 40-acre central precinct surrounded by a palisade. It's clear that the city was strategically designed. The boundaries form a diamond-shape (roughly) with mound groupings at each corner and a central precinct surrounded by a palisade. It measures three miles east to west, and two and one quarter miles north to south for a total of just over five square miles. Canteen Creek flowed from the east and joined Cahokia Creek just north of the central precinct. Cahokia Creek joined the Mississippi eight miles to the west, giving the city direct access to a vast transportation network of mid-continent river systems.

Map of Mississippian sites in mid and southeastern United States.

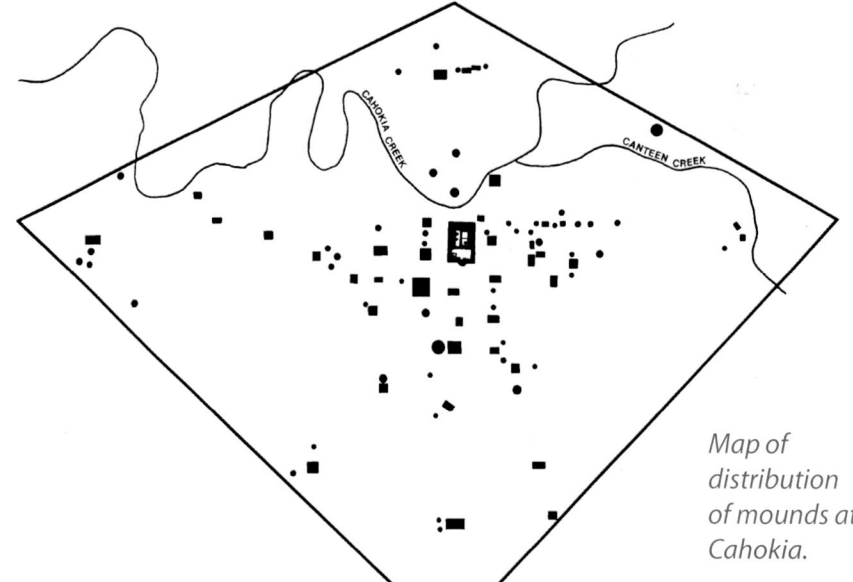

Map of distribution of mounds at Cahokia.

The Cahokian Community

The Political organization of the Cahokian settlement is difficult to determine without a written language. Significant differences in status has been suggested by observed burial practices and grave goods. It is possible that the community was highly stratified, meaning there were elite individuals and commoners and many levels of the hierarchy in between. These may have consisted of advisors, community leaders, clan heads, craft specialists and farmers. An alternative perspective is that it was less stratified with a greater emphasis on kinship. The family unit was important and the community was likely organized into clans or kinship-based units whose community duties were divided based on gender, age, or status.

Sustaining such a large population required year-round work and was dependent on large quantities of cultivated crops and foods that could be gathered from nearby plants and animals, which flourished in the riverine environments and forested areas. Cahokians grew crops, gathered nuts, fruit, and berries, fished the local waterways, harvested various migratory birds and hunted game.

A sedentary lifestyle and a surplus of food allowed for other activities such as arts, games, or crafts, which may have been otherwise spent on subsistence-related activities. Cahokians used rattles, drums, flutes and whistles. They played games of chance with dice and shells, and skill games like ring and pin, in which a player holds a sharp stick tethered by string to a series of deer toes or a perforated leather pad and swings the latter in an arc and tries to skewer the bones or pad to score points (similar to our cup and ball game). The large-scale sport at Cahokia was chunkey, a contest in which two players threw javelin-like sticks at a rolling, concave stone, attempting to be closest to where the stone would stop. The entire community was engaged in this betting game as matches likely occurred throughout the day either in the

Chunkey stones.

Chunkey player pipe made of Missouri flintclay.

Grand Plaza or one of the other plazas situated around the site.

Based on recent excavations at the site, we know that there were members of the community who specialized in the production of certain crafts. The fine examples in pottery, flintknapping, and shell object fabrication that have been recovered at the site indicate that there were masters of various craft industries at Cahokia. Marine shell caches and thousands of shell beads have been recovered in excavations as well as fragments of finely engraved shell cups.

Ongoing research, at a location just beneath of Mound 34, reveals interesting metalworking activities that connect Cahokia to many Mississippian communities in the American Southeast. Here, at about AD 1200, when the population of Cahokia proper was declining and activities shifted to the Ramey Plaza (an area about 430 yards east of Monks Mound), copper-working activities and

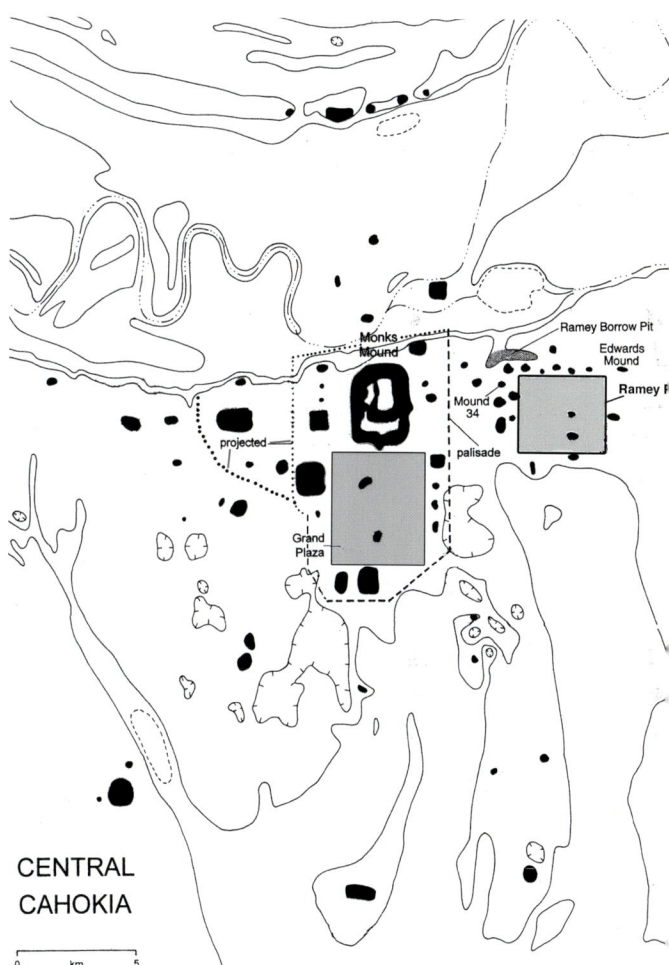

Map showing the location of the Ramey Plaza.

ritual feasting occurred prior to the construction of Mound 34.

Today, Mound 34 is an inconspicuous platform mound about 10 feet high situated on the western edge of the Ramey Plaza. Before its construction, this was the location of the only documented copper workshop at Cahokia. Based on the ubiquity of copper-staining of the soil and other associated features, tools, and materials within this structure, archaeologists have concluded

Copper-stained materials from flotation sample of the copper workshop at Mound 34.

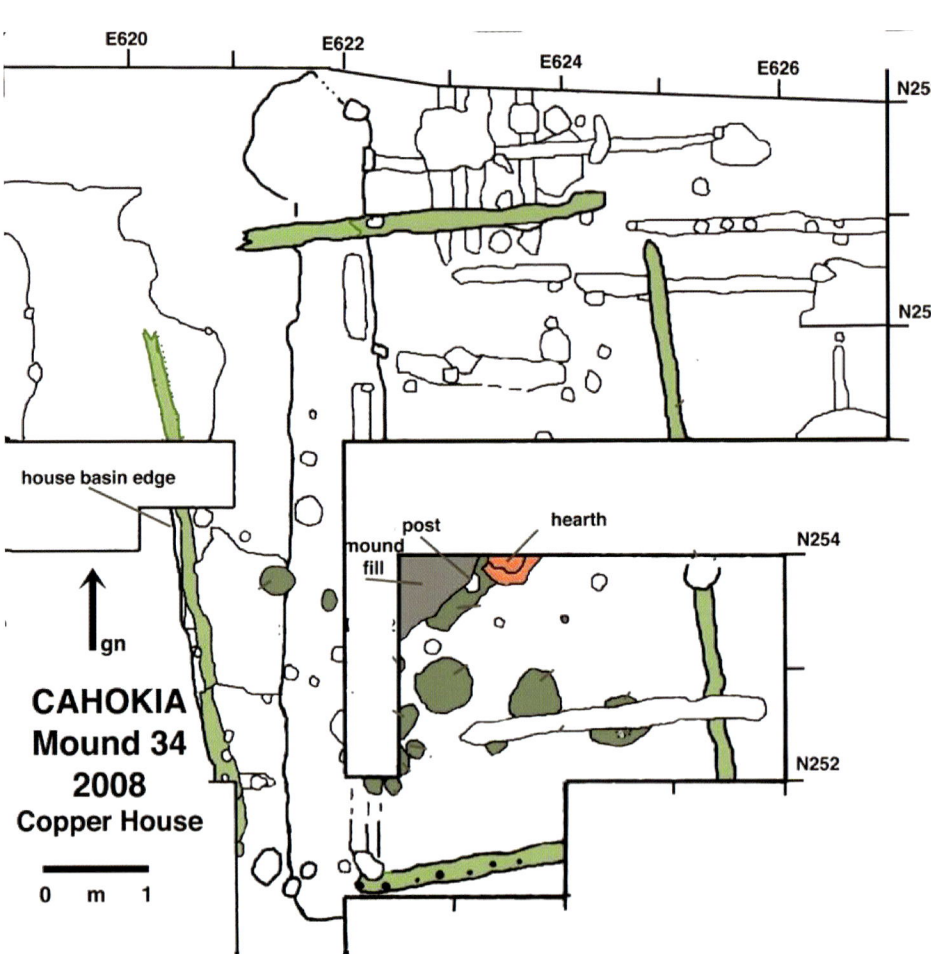

Map depicting copper workshop and associated features. Courtesy John Kelly.

that copper sheet was produced here. Using a technique called cold hammering, the copper nuggets are alternately hammered and annealed (heating the copper to cause a recrystallization of the structure, causing it become malleable again). This process was repeated until the desired thinness was achieved. It is unclear what objects were being produced at the workshop, however, but possibilities include thin repoussé copper plates with symbolic designs, hair and ceremonial costume ornaments, etc. Rolls of copper sheet, some less than one millimeter thick, were found among the grave goods deposited in a ritual burial at Cahokia's Mound 72. Some archaeologists believe that embossed copper plates found at other Mississippian sites were originally made at Cahokia. Following the copper activities, the workshop was then filled in and Mound 34 was constructed over it.

◄ *Copper Wulfing Plate depicting Mississippian icongraphy, made of thin copper sheet.*

Part of the mural in the new exhibit that shows women working in the fields. One is hoeing squash, while the other is gathering sunflower heads. Also depicted to the far left is maize.

Subsistence

Cahokians practiced a diverse agricultural system, relying on a variety of plants that were harvested at different times throughout the year. Archaeologists refer to this ancient agricultural system as the Eastern Agricultural Complex.

15

The Eastern Agricultural Complex

FOR NATIVE AMERICANS LIVING IN EASTERN NORTH AMERICA, THE shift from a solely hunting and gathering subsistence to intensive agriculture took over 4,000 years. This transition was a long and complex process, which emphasizes why plant domestication is seen as one of the greatest achievements of early societies. The change began with the *emergence* of the Eastern Agricultural Complex, which refers to the selection of domesticated indigenous seed plants and their cultivation by Native Americans. Archaeologists are able to trace changes in human behavior by examining domestic habitation patterns as well as the physical attributes of the charred ancient seeds. Physical changes in seeds can be evidence of domestication because they are the results of selective pressure exerted by humans. In some seeds these physical changes often include an increase is seed size, as well as a decrease in seed coat thickness.

These are the seven plants that make up the Eastern Agricultural Complex. This list gives their common and Latin names:

Squash (*Cucurbita pepo*)
Little Barley (*Hordeum pusillum*)
Goosefoot or **Lambsquarter** (*Chenopodium berlandieri*)
Erect Knotweed (*Polygonum erectum*)
Maygrass (*Phalaris caroliniana*)
Sumpweed or Marsh Elder (*Iva annua*)
Sunflower (*Helianthus annuus*)

Maygrass (Phalaris caroliniana). *Photo courtesy of Gail E. Wagner.*

Erect Knotweed (Polygonum erectum). *Photo courtesy of Natalie Mueller.*

This photo shows the difference between the size and shape of the achenes of (from left to right) wild sunflower, archaeological domesticated sunflower, and modern domesticated sunflower. Note the differences. Photo courtesy of Kenneth J. Keller and Washington University in St. Louis.

While these seven plants are often listed together, there are several differences between the species. For example some plants were fully domesticated, while others were cultivated. Domesticated crops are physically different than their wild version. They typically have larger seeds, thinner seed coats, and grow larger seed clusters. Cultivated crops are intentionally grown and tended by humans, but they remain physically the same as their wild versions. These seven plants of the Eastern Agricultural Complex were extremely important in the subsistence and ceremonial practices of Native Americans. The long process began between 3,000 and 2,000 BC, when the first native plant species were domesticated. Centuries later (between 250 BC and AD 200) a shift towards food production economies emerged, which is seen from evidence in the archaeological assemblages. Six to nine centuries after this intensification, maize was introduced and rose to its dominance in the fields (AD 800 to 1100).

Corn (*Zia mays*) was introduced to the American Bottom as early as AD 200. However, its cultivation did not intensify until around AD 800. At this early stage corn was still grown alongside the native domesticates of the Eastern Agricultural Complex. While squash factored significantly in the early formation of Cahokia, beans were not introduced to the central Mississippi Valley until after Cahokia's decline. Plant cultivation centered on indigenous cultigens as well as corn. Due to the difference in preservation, it is difficult to know what percentage each plant played in Cahokians' diet. Corn was a more productive plant, but the native domesticates were more nutritious. By growing both corn and indigenous crops, Cahokia was able to feed more people while also maintaining nutritional variety.

Archaeologists have discovered a number of female flintclay figurines around the greater Cahokia area. The characters depicted call to mind important Earth Mother traditions, which were told and recorded by later tribes.

Westbrook Pipe, found in Desha County, Arkansas. This flintclay figurine depicts Old-Woman-Who-Never-Dies. Growing from her hands are two crop plants, most likely one of the Eastern Agricultural Complex plants. She sits in front of a basket or bundle that is seen on other figurines and is believed to represent a sacred bundle.

The figures that are discovered around the American Bottom are interpreted as the ancestral being known as "Old-Woman-Who-Never-Dies" or "Grandmother." She had powers of rebirth and was also able to control the weather. The female gender is often associated with rebirth, giving of life, and agriculture. While men may have helped to initially clear the fields, women and girls labored to plant, weed, and harvest the crops. Below is a Mandan (North Dakota) legend (Judson 2007) that tells of Old-Woman-Who-Never-Dies and her important role in providing subsistence for people. This is a later legend, so corn is predominately mentioned, but during Cahokia's time of power, this ancestral being would have guarded over all crops, indigenous ones as well as maize.

Mississippians shared a fundamental belief system that gave meaning to their lives and order to the universe. This can be seen in cultural materials that they left be-

Old-Woman-Who-Never-Dies

IN THE SUN LIVES THE LORD OF LIFE. IN THE MOON LIVES OLD-WOMAN-Who-Never-Dies. She has six children, three sons and three daughters. These live in the sky. The eldest son is Day; another is the Sun; another is Night. The eldest daughter is the Morning Star, called "The Woman Who Wears a Plume"; another is a star, which circles around the polar star, and she is called "The Striped Gourd"; the third is Evening Star.

Every spring Old-Woman-Who-Never-Dies sends the wild geese, the swans, and the ducks. When she sends the wild geese, the Indians plant their corn and Old-Woman-Who-Never-Dies makes it grow. When eleven wild geese are found together, the Indians know the corn crop will be very large. The swans mean that the Indians must plant gourds; the ducks, that they must plant beans.

Indians always save dried meat for these wild birds, so when they come in the spring they may have a corn feast. They build scaffolds of many poles, three or four rows, and one above the others. On this they hang the meat. Then the old women in the village, each one with a stick, meet around the scaffold. In one end of the stick is an ear of corn. Sitting in a circle, they plant their sticks in the ground in front of them. Then they dance around the scaffolds while the old men beat the drums and rattle the gourds. Afterwards the old women in the village are allowed to eat the dried meat.

In the fall they hold another corn feast, after the corn is ripe. This is so that Old-Woman-Who-Never-Dies may send the buffalo herds to them. Each woman carries the entire cornstalk, with the ears attached, just as it was pulled up by the roots. Then they call on Old-Woman-Who-Never-Dies and say, "Mother, pity us. Do not send the cold too soon, or we may not have enough meat. Mother, do not let the game depart, so that we may have enough for winter."

In the fall, when the birds go south to Old-Woman, they take back the dried meat hung on the scaffolds, because Old-Woman is very fond of it.

Old-Woman-Who-Never-Dies has large patches of corn, kept for her by the great stag and by the white-tailed stag. Blackbirds also help her guard her corn patches. The corn patches are large, therefore the Old-Woman has the help also of the mice and the moles. In the spring the birds go back north, back to Old-Man-Who-Never-Dies.

In the olden time, Old-Woman-Who-Never-Dies lived near the Little Missouri. Sometimes the Indians visited her. One day twelve came, and she offered them only a small kettle of corn. They were very hungry and the kettle was very small. But as soon as it was empty, it at once became filled again, so all the Indians had enough to eat.

Birger Figurine. This female figurine holds the head of a feline-faced serpent and hoes its back. Its body splits into squash vines growing up her back.

hind as well as features and activities. Symbols and iconography found on objects such as the Birdman Tablet found in the East Lobes excavation on Monks Mound, or the Wulfing plates found in Dunklin County,

Birdman Tablet, engraved sandstone, found at excavations on Monks Mound.

Missouri, are part of a body of symbols and icons that Mississippians used to express their beliefs, many of which probably have antecedents at Cahokia.

At Cahokia, Mound 72 reveals much about certain mortuary rituals, details about the social stratification of their society, and about their economic system, but more importantly, the complex of burials at Mound 72 reveals details about their belief in an afterlife. Mound 72 is an unassuming ridgetop mound about 6 feet tall. In 1967, a five-year excavation began, led by Dr. Melvin Fowler, which revealed a mortuary display that archaeologists are still trying to fully understand. Mound 72 was built over three smaller mounds that covered various burials and grave goods, including the remains of over 280 people, some of whom appear to be sacrificed and buried in mass graves. The most intriguing of the mortuary display is what we call the "beaded burial." The remains of an important male resting

The "Beaded Burial" exhibit in the Interpretive Center gallery.

Interpretive painting of Mound 72 burial activites. Illustration by Herb Roe, ©2013.

on a blanket of about 20,000 marine-shell beads forming the shape of a hawk or other raptor. This individual was surrounded by attendants and near him were phenomenal grave goods. Based on the different Mound 72 burials (some headless and handless, some disarticulated, some on litters, mostly young women, etc.), their orientations, and the grave offerings, it appears as if a grand ritual event was carried out, sometime around AD 1050, in association with the death of a significant person.

Mound 72 Offerings

ONE OF THE MOST INTRIGUING CHARACTERISTICS OF MOUND 72 and the Beaded Burial was the copious amount of goods or "offerings" that were part of the mortuary event. The goods that were very deliberately placed inside the grave were exotic and pristine (in most cases). Mica is a translucent and reflective sheet silicate mineral. The nearest source for this smoky fragile mineral was likely the Smoky Mountains region of North Carolina. There were nearly two bushels of this material in its raw state in the Mound 72 offering. Next to the mica were 15 chunkey stones. There were also rolls of copper about three feet long, as well as marine shell beads. Two piles of arrow points were carefully placed, one pile of 332 points was oriented west-northwest, and the other of 413 points was oriented east-southeast. The points were bundled together in groups representing different material sources as well as styles. Beneath the submounds were more artifact caches, including over 36,000 shell beads, more than 400 arrow points, hundreds of bone and antler arrow points, various other materials, as well as some ritually-broken pottery.

Group of finely crafted arrow points from Mound 72.

Twin Mounds

TWO PAIRS OF MOUNDS AT THE SITE, EACH CONSISTING OF ONE conical mound and one platform mound, are intriguing based on the nature of their paired construction. The larger of the pair, known as the Twin Mounds (Fox Mound and Roundtop Mound), are situated at the southern end of the Grand Plaza, directly opposite of Monks Mound and inside of the Palisade wall. The other pair, the Little Twin Mounds, are located southwest of the Twin Mounds and west of a large borrow pit. Although neither pair has been excavated, testing around them has determined that each pair was constructed on a platform that joined them. A causeway was evident that connected the two mounds, fur-

The Twin Mounds situated directly opposite Monks Mound in the Grand Plaza.

thering the interpretation that the two serve a "paired" function. In previous periods, conical mounds were commonly burial mounds. It has been suggested that these pairs could serve a mortuary function, with the platform mound supporting some type of charnel structure and the conical mound serving as a burial mound, based on excavations elsewhere.

Mounds and Plazas

The earthen mounds that dot the landscape, (about 80 of the original 120 survive), are perhaps the most obvious landscape feature that remains of the archaeological site. These mounds vary in size, shape, and function. While the mounds vary greatly in size and shape, generally there are three types of mounds found at the site: flat-topped pyramids called temple or platform mounds; conical mounds; and linear ridgetop mounds. Some are paired, like the Twin Mounds found at the south end of the Grand Plaza, directly opposite from Monks Mound, or the Little Twin Mounds found just southwest of their larger namesake. Clusters of several mounds grouped together are found in various locations at the site. Most were modified over time, constructed in several phases, and some may have been repurposed.

Platform mounds are the most common type of mounds found at the site. These mounds are flat-topped and mostly rectangular in shape, though some are square. They vary in height,

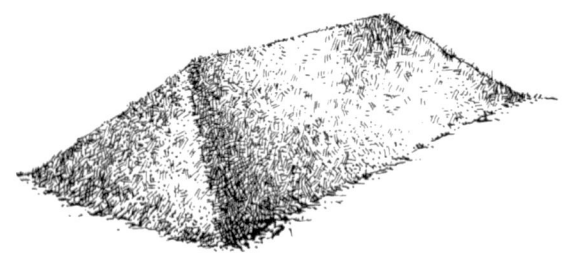

RIDGETOP

CONICAL

PLATFORM

ranging from only a few feet to the 100-foot Monks Mound. It's difficult to say with certainty what the function of these mounds were, but it is believed that they supported important structures, such as government buildings, religious structures, homes of the elite, council lodges, or other significant public places.

Conical mounds are circular and come to a point or are dome-shaped. These mounds most likely serve a mortuary function based on the preponderance of these mounds used in the previous period for this purpose. No archaeology has been conducted on the conical mounds at the site to confirm this.

Ridgetop mounds are the least common at the site. There are at least six that are readily identifiable. These mounds are rectangular at the base and longer than they are wide, and the sides slope up to form a peak on the top similar to the gables of a roof. The fact that the two largest ridgetop mounds (Powell Mound and Rattlesnake Mound) lie at the west and south boundaries of the site and that they are oriented along an east-west axis has led some to suggest that they served as intentional markers of the city's limits. However some contain burials, and Mound 72, a ridgetop mound oriented northwest to southeast, is located near the center of the site, and is the scene of a very complex mortuary event with multiple mass burials of obvious high status.

Monks Mound dominates the site as the largest mound and occupies the center of the city plan. It is clearly the epicenter of importance both spatially and socially now as it undoubtedly was during the Mississippian period. At 100 feet tall, it is the largest prehistoric earthen mound in the Americas. Due to erosion and various changes

◀ *The three mound types found at Cahokia. Sketch by Albert Meyer.*

How Were They Built

EXCAVATIONS AT THE SITE SHOW THAT THE EARTHEN MOUNDS WERE CONstructed by digging soil from various locations at the site, what we now call borrow pits, and nearby creek bottoms, using stone and wooden tools. The soils were then hauled to the construction site in a basket or a bag and either set in a pile as a "basket load" or spread out in a thin layer, in a "broadcasting" method. In some cases, sod blocks were cut and used in the construction process as well. These basket loads are easily identified in excavations and archaeologists have concluded that one basket load weighed about 40 – 60 lbs. The soils used in the construction process varied in composition and color, some silty, clayey and dark, some sandy and light in color, and often a mixture of these. The visible differences in the soils often make the basket loads easily identifiable.

Excavation unit at East Lobe of Monks Mound shows evidence of basket loads.

View of Monks Mound looking north across the Grand Plaza.

to the structure, the basal dimensions are difficult to determine but originally it likely covered about 14 acres which is larger at its base than the Great Pyramid of Cheops in Egypt.

Archaeology conducted on the Fourth Terrace of Monks Mound in the mid-1960s and early 1970s revealed that a building measuring 104 by 48 feet once occupied its summit. This possible temple was so large that it required several deep post pits for roof supports. The small amount of artifacts within and around the structure indicates that whatever the function, it was deliberately kept clean and free of debris or artifacts, unlike other structures found on the site which are associated with storage and the refuse from every-day residential use.

The mounds may be the most obvious but were not the only great architectural feat accomplished by the Cahokians. There are several plazas situated around the site that required skill and a fundamental understanding of engineering principles. These were level open spaces, and generally free of dwellings, used for community events and ritual gatherings. Four plazas surround Monks Mound, one in each cardinal direction. Its southern plaza, the Grand Plaza, is by far the largest at Cahokia Mounds. The Cahokians created this 40-acre space by cutting and filling the undulating landscape to create a level area stretching from Monks Mound on the north to the Twin Mounds on the south. The entire surface was then capped with a sandy soil. It is surrounded on all sides by mounds, with two situated inside the plaza. The Grand Plaza served as a public space for the Cahokians. It likely was used for important gatherings, community events, and as a playing field for games.

Structure

The Cahokians were accomplished builders. They constructed a variety of structures throughout the site using readily available resources. Granaries, sacred structures, compounds, stockades or palisades, and sun calendars are some of the structures that have been identified, though the most common structures were single-family dwellings. Most of the dwellings had one entryway and were about 200-400 square-feet or smaller. The largest structures was the 5,000 square-foot structure situated on top of Monks Mound. All of these were constructed with precision and sometimes reconstructed, varying slightly in size from its predecessor. Excavations on the Interpretive Center tract, revealed over 80 buildings of varying types.

The method used to construct dwellings and other similar structures was simple and practical. A framework of wooden poles was set into dug trenches (the classic Mississippian wall-trench construction method). Once the framework was set, the trenches were filled in with dirt and each section was lashed together with saplings. Sometimes, small saplings (wattle) were woven around the wall posts and the walls were plastered with daub, a mixture of clay and grass. Most house walls were probably covered with layers of woven mats. Roofs were steeply pitched and thatched with bundled grasses that were harvested from local prairies.

Illustration of granary.

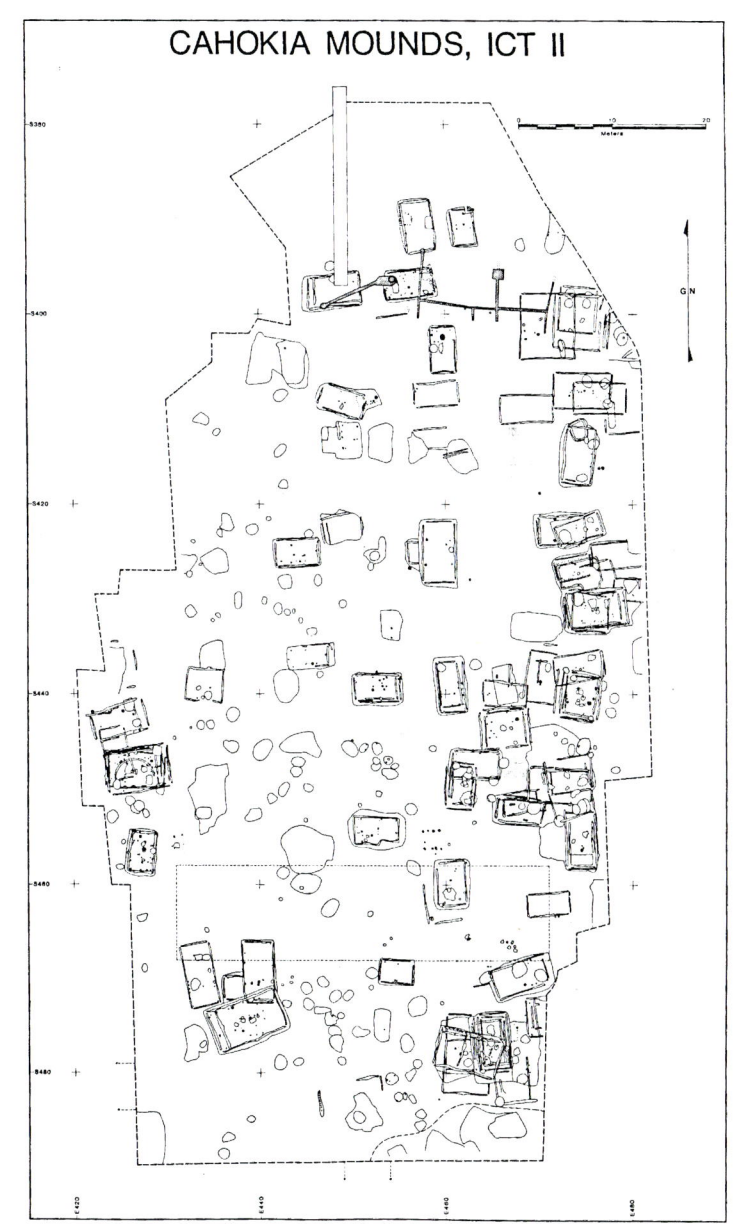

Plan map of rectangular structures, pits, and other features of the excavation from the Interpretive Center. ▶

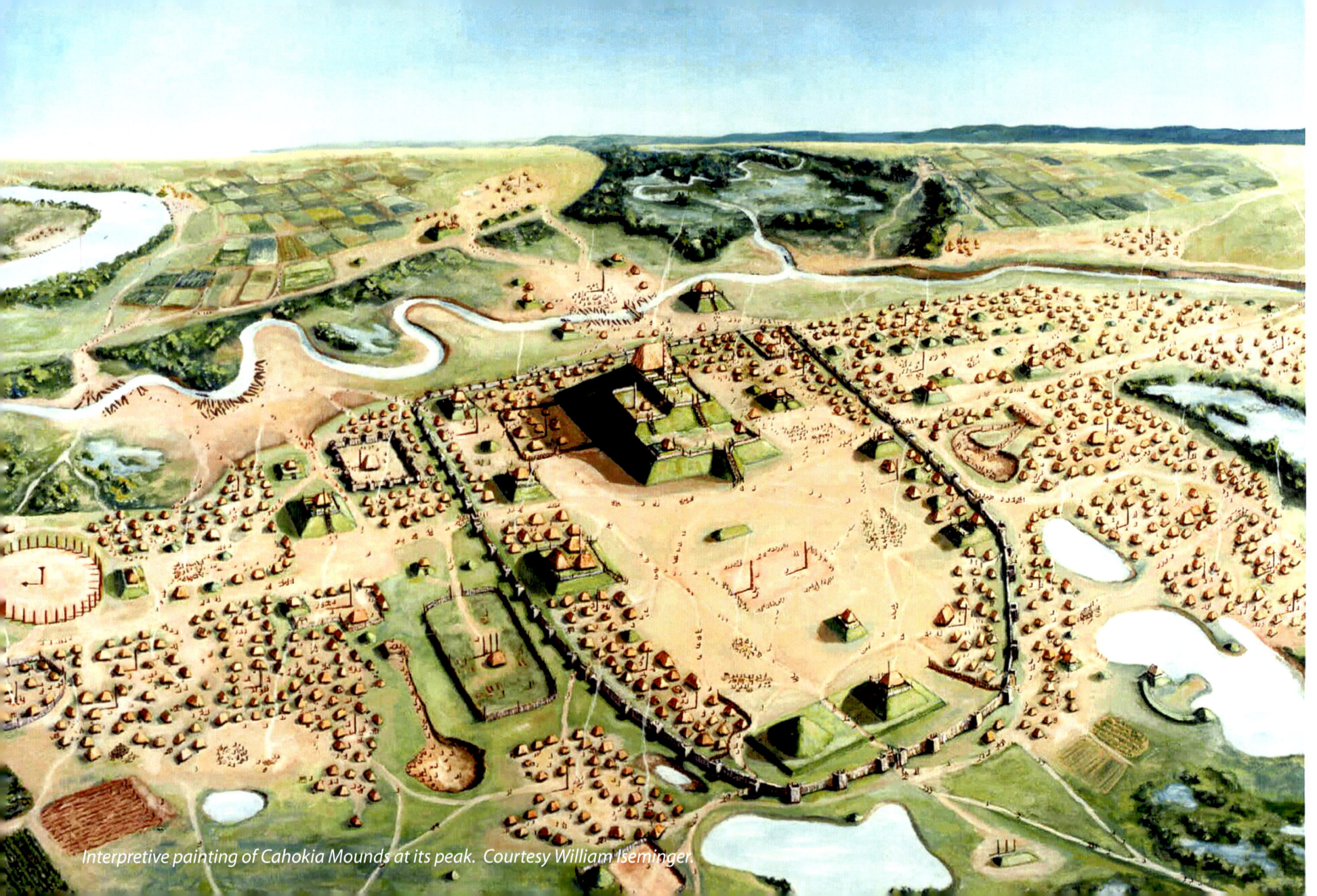

Interpretive painting of Cahokia Mounds at its peak. Courtesy William Iseminger.

Beginning with excavations in the 1960s by the Illinois State Museum, and recently revisited by University of Bologna/Washington University students, some intriguing structures in the West Plaza have been identified and require more investigations. Referred to as "compounds," these large square and round enclosures, one with regularly-spaced circular bastions, begs some intriguing questions. There is no obvious evidence that these square compounds, measuring about 80 feet by 80 feet, were roofed. The bastions (or rooms) indicate that what was occurring within the walls was guarded, either to protect what was inside or keep it shielded from the outside.

The two-mile long Stockade (sometimes referred to as the Palisade Wall) was first identified in aerial photographs taken of the area in the 1920s and 1930s. Excavations in 1966 confirmed that there was a wall surrounding the central portion of the city, enclosing Monks Mound, the Grand Plaza, and 17 other mounds. This "Central Ceremonial Precinct" was protected by this 10-12-foot tall wall, with bastions about 90 feet apart. Construction of this wall, and its subsequent repairs and reconstructions, is associated with a marked shift in organization at the site. This shift occurred from AD 1175-1275, during the late Stirling/Moorehead phases, a time of political change and population decline. It was a monumental architectural feat that required some 15,000-20,000 oak and hickory logs, each measuring about one foot in diameter. The stockade could have served as a social barrier as well as a defensive structure against either real or perceived threats.

One of the most fascinating structures found at the site was the sun calendar we now call Woodhenge (although there were five versions of it).

These large wooden-post circular structures were used to mark the rising sun, especially at the equinoxes and solstices, and

Interpretive painting of construction of Woodhenge by L.K. Townsend.

probably other important dates in their ritual calendar. The post-pits that defined several circles were first discovered in the early 1960s by Dr. Warren Wittry, hired by the Illinois State Museum to conduct archaeology as part of the proposed Interstate 255 project. After more archaeology was conducted in subsequent excavations, Dr. Wittry had identified many of the post-pits for five calendar circles. The first circle consisted of 24 posts and was 240 feet in diameter. The subsequent circles to its west were roughly in the same location but with the center of each slightly shifted from its predecessor. In addition to the shift in location, each subsequent circle was increased in size, by adding 12 posts (36, 48, 60) with the final version being only the eastern arc of posts that aligned with sunrises but if it had been complete it would have had 72 posts. These large solar circles were an important feature to the Cahokians. They not only identified key periods of the seasons but also were likely areas for important rituals or ceremonies that were closely tied to these seasons. The third Woodhenge of 48 posts has been reconstructed at the original location and is 410 feet in diameter.

Decline

During the twelfth century, the peak development of Cahokia Mounds occurred. Towards the end of this episode, things started to change. This was likely when the slow decline of the large city began. From limited excavations, we can tell that around this time some public areas were returned to residential areas, the large building on top of Monks Mound was dismantled and the summit was covered with over four feet of earth, and activities were localized to smaller portions of the site. The Ramey Plaza, a large plaza located east of Monks Mound, is surrounded by small mounds on

Dr. Warren Wittry with a section of a Red Cedar post from Woodhenge.

all sides and became a center of activity at the site. The grandeur of large-scale monumental architecture and the associated activities seems to have been replaced by a less-conspicuous occupation focused on ritual activities. People began to leave the site and move to outlying areas, either starting new communities or joining existing ones. By around AD 1350 the site was nearly abandoned. There is no clear answer to what led to the decline and eventual abandonment. While theories abound, it was likely a combination of factors that led to the decline. Resource depletion, landscape degradation, climate shifts, warfare or political instabilities were some of the factors that could have been involved. Rather than a mass exodus from the site, it was a slow decline, lasting several generations, with some people continuing to thrive in the region. After AD 1300 people from the north began to move into the region.

The portion of the site that is within the State Historic Site boundary is protected and is no longer in danger of contemporary destruction. Therefore, only a limited number of small, controlled excavations are conducted on the site. Even though excavations are limited, new information gleaned from research on the site and at neighboring sites continues to expand our knowledge of the culture, as well as environmental factors that likely played a role in the city's eventual demise.

Map showing the location of the Ramey Plaza. ▶

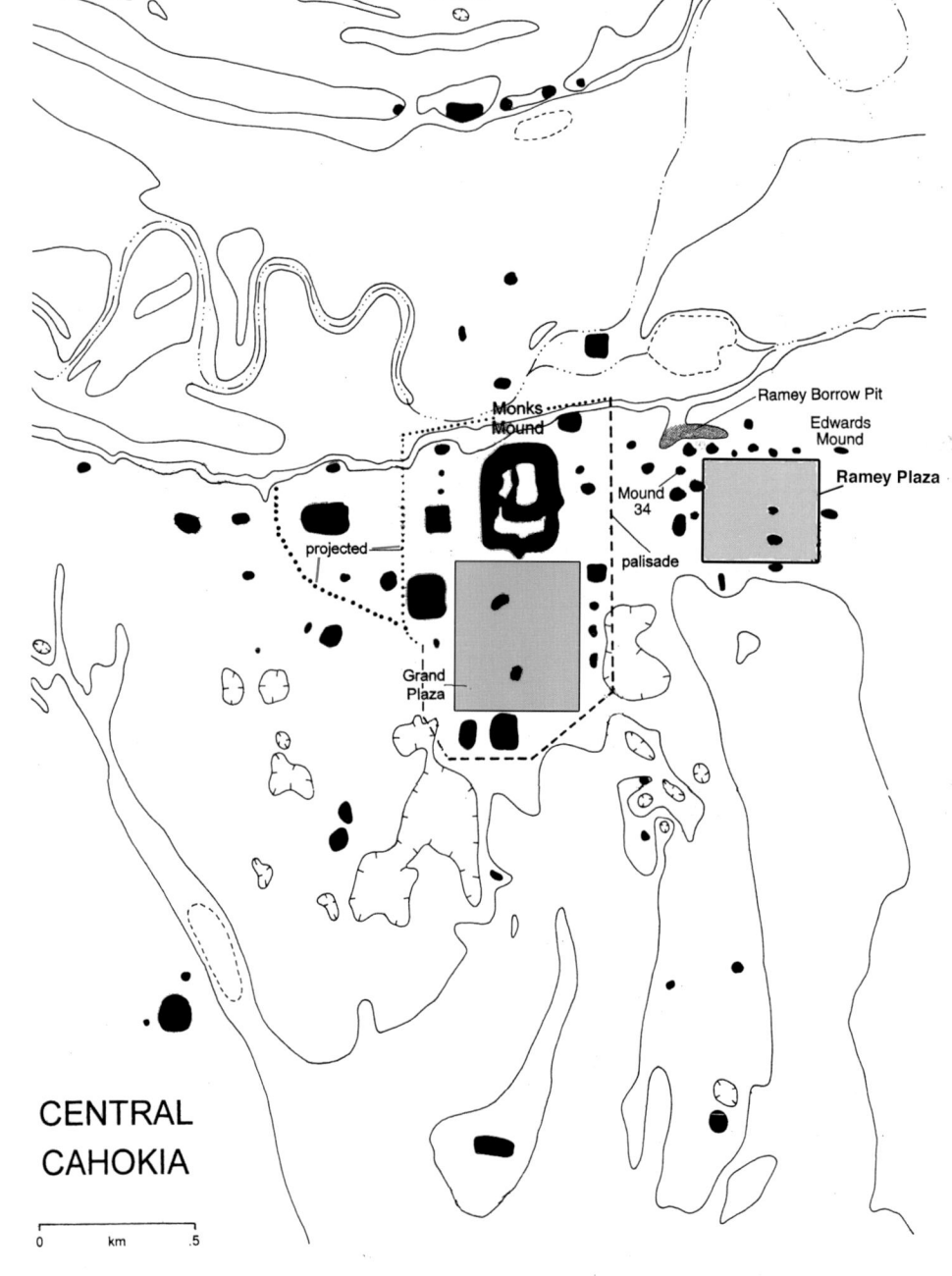

Cahokia Mounds Today

The Cahokia Mounds State Historic Site today is comprised of 2100 acres of the central portion of the archaeological site (including 74 partial or full mounds of the original 120), and a comprehensive Interpretive Center with an exhibit gallery. The iPod tours, life-sized city diorama, 17-minute orientation show, and exhibit and artifact islands bring the Mississippian culture to life. A large-scale, plan-view model of the site, murals depicting interpretations of the site during its peak, and the panoramic window view of Monks Mound and the Grand Plaza provide a unique experience for visitors. Over 250,000 people from every state and about 80 countries around the world visit the site annually. The site is a U.S. National Historic Landmark, and United Nations Educational and Scientific Organization World Heritage Site.

Village scene from Interpretive Center life-sized village.

Interpretive Center at Cahokia Mounds State Historic Site.

Gallery exhibit from the Interpretive Center at Cahokia Mounds State Historic Site.

AN AMAZING DISCOVERY

In the Spring of 2008, two strong low-pressure centers dragged moisture from the Gulf of Mexico and produced wide-scale, Midwest flooding. The resulting record rainfalls, and periods of extended river flooding, wreaked havoc from Texas to Indiana. In the late spring, when the floodwaters began to recede in Cross County, Arkansas, Matthew Guth stumbled upon a treasure. He discovered a 700-year old, baldcypress dugout canoe resting on a sandbar of one of the St. Francis River meanders. What he found was a remnant of America's past, a physical manifestation of the ingenuity and skill of a people from long ago, patiently awaiting its final destination as the centerpiece of a large exhibit at, arguably, the most significant and, without a doubt, the largest archaeological site in North America, Cahokia Mounds State Historic Site.

Mr. Guth recovered the canoe, and with the help of friends, moved it to his house in Wynne, Arkansas. Knowing that he needed to keep the wood wet, he found a shady spot, put tarps down, continuously doused it, and kept it covered. Suspecting that he had a unique piece of American history, perhaps dating to the 19th or 18th century, he contacted Jeffrey Mitchem, Ph.D. from the Parkin Research Station of the Arkansas Archaeological Survey to find the answers to his questions: How old was it? Was it authentic? Was it Native American? Who has legal ownership? Mr. Guth worked with Dr. Mitchem over the course of the next year to ensure the canoe was fully researched, conserved, and claimed its rightful place among America's history.

Upon careful analyses by Dr. Mitchem, and other state park employees, it was noted that the canoe was exceptionally well-preserved, largely due to the anaerobic (relating to an absence of free oxygen) environment of the river bottom. It was almost completely intact, but a crack ran almost the entire length of the bottom. The

Ancient canoe found by Matt Guth along the St. Francis River.

weight of the canoe is difficult to discern, but it is heavier at the stern than it is at the bow. It measures 21.9 feet long, 10.25 inches in depth, and 21.25 inches wide at the top, and 13 inches wide at the bottom (on average). The thickness of the hull varies between 1.38 and 1.75 inches. Steven Boles, Research Archaeologist, Illinois State Archaeological Survey, has conducted research on the canoe and has concluded, this dugout would have handled quite well on large, fast rivers with the ability to quickly dodge obscure obstacles such as floating logs and root wads. Steve states, "When viewing the dugout from the side, the hull profile is referred to as the rocker (the amount of curvature of the hull). How a dugout will handle depends a great deal on the degree of curvature or slope at the end. The sloped ends of the dugout would be considered a pronounced rocker, indicating it was designed for high maneuverability. The hull between the ends is flat and the sides are gently arched. This design provides a shallow draft and combines enhanced stability with efficiency, and speed."

There were clear tool marks, plus charred areas, indicating the manufacture technique included the burn-and-scrape method. While still in Arkansas, a small section was removed for potential radiocarbon dating. With the funds donated by Mr. Guth, the sample was sent to Beta Analytic. It was determined that the

Ancient canoe bow showing char marks.

Area of canoe removed for radiocarbon dating.

Interior of canoe showing lengthwise crack.

Radiocarbon Dating

LEARNING THE AGE OF AN ARTIFACT IS IMPORTANT FOR PLACING IT IN ITS PROPER cultural context. It can also help date archaeological sites. There are several radiometric methods, measuring of radioactive isotopes and their decay products, that can be used for dating. One of the most widely used for dating most organic materials is radiocarbon dating.

Carbon is a ubiquitous element found all around us. It's in the air, in our food, in plants and animals. It's composed of atoms, which are composed of particles called protons, electrons, and neutrons. An isotope is a different version of an element that has a unique number of neutrons. Carbon comes in three varieties, or isotopes, C12, C13, and C14. C12 and C13 are stable isotopes but C14 is unstable and breaks down easily when bombarded with cosmic rays. When unstable isotopes breakdown, radiation is emitted. This process is called radioactive decay.

As living things consume plants and animals, they consume the radioactive carbon in them. When a living thing dies, the uptake of carbon stops, and C14 begins to decay. It takes 5,730 years for half of the C14 to change to Nitrogen; this is known as the half-life of C14. After another 5,730 years, only one quarter of the original C14 will remain, and so on. By measuring this C14, scientists can determine the date of death of an organic artifact or ecofact within a range of 40-200 years.

continued ▶

Radiocarbon Dating continued...

As with any method, C14 dating isn't ideal for every situation. The relatively short half-life of C14, makes it reliable only up to about 75,000 years. Another limitation with using this dating method is that when dating wood, there is a chance that the wood was dead for quite some time prior to its use by people and its entrance in the archaeological record. This makes it difficult to date an archaeological site using only this method.

C14 dating can be a useful tool in dating artifacts and other archaeological remains, however, it would be best utilized by combining it with other dating methods. Historic records, dendrochronology, other radiometric methods, or diagnostic materials from the site, that are identical to materials from other sites that have already been dated, are other methods that can be combined with C14 dating.

calibrated (2-sigma) date ranges were cal AD 1310-1360 and cal AD 1380-1450, about 500 years prior to the initial estimates. Dr. David Stahle, of the Department of Geosciences at the University of Arkansas, determined that the canoe was made of bald cypress (*Taxodium distichum*), a species with a natural resistance to rotting and other characteristics making it a good material for canoes.

Luckily for Mr. Guth, and the canoe, it was found on a sandbar. If the canoe had been found on one of the banks, the adjacent landowner would have ownership rights. If it had been found in the stream, the State would have been the legal owners. But since it was found on a sandbar, the finder was the legal owner of the property.

With this new information, Mr. Guth began to contact individuals and organizations he thought would be interested in acquiring the canoe. A few organizations in Illinois and elsewhere expressed interest in acquiring it, but the preservation promised to be both labor-intensive and expensive, making the acquisition less-than-palatable for many. A few months later, Dr. Mitchem received a call from Dr. Mark Esarey, Site Superintendent of Cahokia Mounds State Historic Site, who expressed interest in acquiring the canoe. Dr. Esarey inquired about the legal ownership of the canoe and if there were other interested parties. He explained that the Illinois State Archaeological Society (ISAS) was considering purchasing the canoe and donating it to Cahokia Mounds, but wanted to be certain that there were no other interested parties. He assured all concerned that the site was committed to conserving the artifact and displaying it in the museum gallery where it would contribute to the interpretation of indigenous inhabitants of the Midwest. In this new home, the canoe would be accessible to the roughly 250,000 visitors to the UNESCO World Heritage Site and U.S. National Historic Landmark each year. In February of 2009, ISAS purchased the canoe and donated it to Cahokia Mounds. Never wavering in the face of a challenge, a well-planned and extensive conservation effort was put in place by the Cahokia Mounds staff.

The first challenge, was how to transport the canoe to Cahokia Mounds. Not only was it 21.9 ft. long and weighed about 700 lbs., but the wood was very fragile. When hardwoods are waterlogged, the anaerobic environment leads to a profound chemical change and alteration of the composition, even though the form and shape are retained. The bacterial action breaks down much of the water-soluble substances in the cells resulting in a more porous material. These pores then fill with water, maintaining the shape of the object. Once the wood is removed from the water, the water evaporates. Since the water is then the only thing holding the cell structures open, the surface tension of the evaporation causes the cell walls to collapse, creating shrinkage and distortion. For this reason, it was imperative to keep the canoe wet while it was being transported to Illinois.

The site rallied the support of local volunteers and the Cahokia Archaeological Society to transport the canoe to its new home. They then drove to Arkansas, equipped with a rented moving

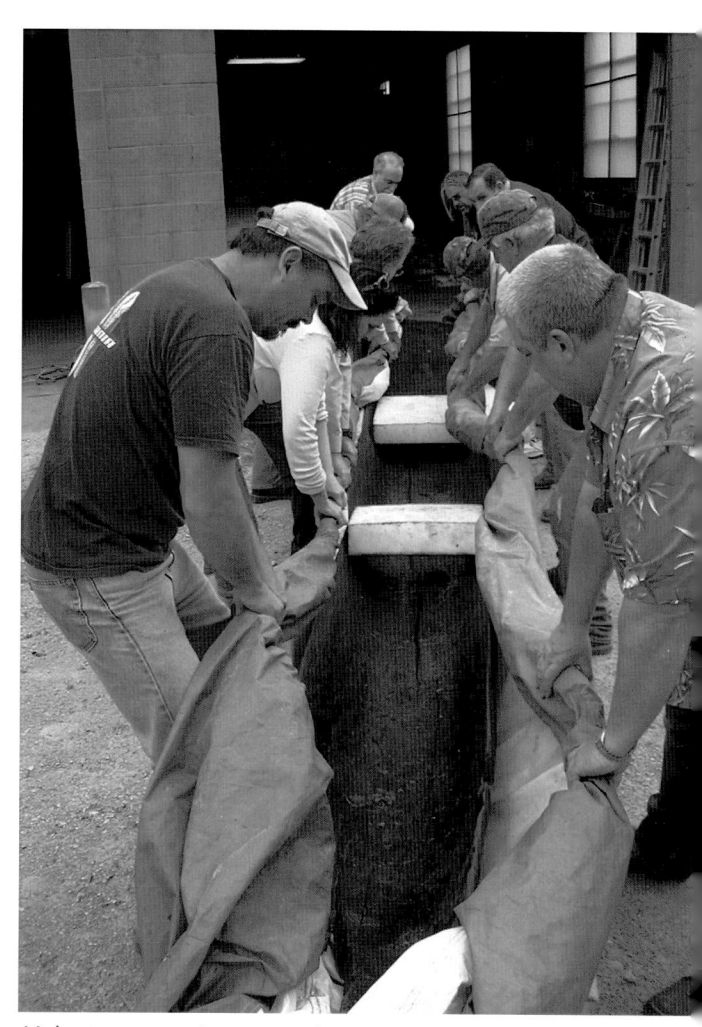

Volunteers moving canoe into storage area.

truck and about a dozen volunteers, and brought the artifact to Cahokia Mounds.

Larry Kinsella, Jim Marlen, Steven Boles, and several site staff members, constructed a wooden trough, which was open on one end, to contain the artifact, and lined it with rubber pond liner. The canoe was carried in a vinyl tarp by about a dozen people and placed inside of the trough. The open end was sealed up and the trough was filled with water.

The first stage of the conservation effort was to submerge the canoe in the vat filled with water to bring it back to the fully waterlogged state and halt the degradation from the evaporating water that occurred during the move. When the canoe was lowered into the vat, it began to float a bit, so the team added weights and braces to keep it fully submerged.

The second phase was the addition of polyethylene glycol (PEG) to preserve the cell structure of the wood. PEG is a synthetic material that ranges in molecular weight. Three weights are generally available with consistency ranging from liquids to a wax-like material. All weights have some properties of waxes, but are distinguished from true waxes by the fact that they are soluble in alcohol and water. The decision was made to use the PEG 400 weight, the lightweight, liquid PEG. A PEG and water solution was added to the vat, along with a circulation pump and a fungicide. The vat temperature was gradually

Vat construction.

Lining the vat.

increased until it reached about 60 degrees Celsius. During this time, PEG percentage of the solution increased as solvent evaporated. During the process, the wax slowly permeated the wood, displacing the water. After a period of about three years, the time it took for the concentration of PEG to reach 70 percent, the canoe was covered with (70-100 percent) molten PEG.

When the end of the conservation process was in sight, around August 2013, conversations were reignited about the development of an exhibit to highlight the canoe and its interconnection with the American Bottom and Mississippian life-ways. At this time, Molly Wawrzyniak, joined the site staff as a Graduate Research Assistant. She began the daunting task of coordinating the new exhibit, which would feature a 52-foot mural and life-sized diorama depicting the American Bottom, with the ancient canoe as the centerpiece.

Canoe Research

Once the task of preserving the canoe and planning the exhibit were underway, questions began to arise regarding its construction, function, and carrying capacity. In an effort to understand the construction process of the ancient canoe, Gene Stratmann, Site Technician, conducted an experimental archaeology project, under the supervision of Bill Iseminger, Assistant Site Manager,

Experimental Archaeology

EXPERIMENTAL ARCHAEOLOGY IS A SCIENTIFIC METHOD used in archaeology to interpret past technologies, behavior, or material culture. This method uses the correct period of tools, materials, and procedures, while scientifically monitoring the reconstruction. Artifacts are not just reproduced, but the processes used in their manufacture are tested and the data is carefully recorded. This data is then used to interpret the past, not just the artifact, but the processes, both cultural and technological, involved in its production. Different levels of investment exist when conducting this type of research, ranging from non-scientific approaches of reconstruction to very detailed scientific reconstruction. Non-scientific approaches include, for example, hobby flint-knapping. This is done by individuals who simply enjoy the process of reconstructing stone tools for their enjoyment and personal education. At the most scientific level, the process is recreated as closely to the original method as possible, using period tools and technologies and following the rules governing scientific methodology and documenting each step of production and use.

and with the help of Lori Belknap. His objective was to determine what the indigenous manufacturing process was in its construction. Mr. Stratmann noticed what appear to be chop marks throughout the canoe and charred areas. Some of the questions he set out to answer were: How much effort was needed to dig out the center of the log using only chopping? Could it have been possible to combine pyrotechnic techniques and chopping? Are the chipped out segments of the canoe the result of chopping? How much time is involved in chopping out the center vs. using pyrotechnic methods?

Mr. Stratmann first made a celt (an axe that fits into a hole at the end of a handle) out of a piece of basalt that he obtained in glacial till about 35 miles north of the site. He used a diamond blade grinder to remove about one inch of the bulk and used a prehistoric pecking method with a hammer stone to finish the shape. He then secured a four-foot section of a pin oak tree, about one and one half-foot in diameter, from a felled tree on the site. Several trials of wood removal were utilized on different sections of the log during the experiment. The chopping method using the celt was the quickest method for removing bulk, but the burn and scrape method was the least labor-intense method. Using a stone wedge to remove bulk was the least effective method as the wedge was not able to penetrate the log. Since there is evidence of both burning and chopping on the artifact canoe, it is evident that both methods were employed depending on the requirements of the design and structural elements of the log. For instance, once the bulk of the interior was burned out and scraped with an adze or a shell, chopping could have been used to shape the exterior or thin out the walls of the gunwale.

Celt and chopped area of experiment by Gene Stratmann.

The carrying capacity of the canoe was of interest considering the variety of canoe shapes and sizes that were manufactured. Carrying capacity is basically the maximum weight capacity based on the gross displaced volume of the boat to the point that flooding will sink the boat. Understanding how much the canoe could transport was important for interpreting the role this canoe played in Mississippian culture. Calculating the carrying capacity of a vessel is complicated and involves a number of factors related to how the watercraft is constructed. Mr. Boles, working with engineer, Scott Morris of Grumman canoes, has determined the carrying capacity, to be about 500 to 600 pounds. Assuming a two-man crew, examples of cargo are 43 – 7 pound deer hides, 150 – 2 pound chert hoes, or 200-300 pounds of corn on the cob. The ancient canoe could also have easily carried four to five crew members depending on their individual weights.

Gene Stratmann conducting a burn and scrape experiment to determine construction methods.

Detail from market painting by Michael Hampshire showing dugout canoes on Cahokia Creek behind Monks Mound.

AN AQUATIC TRADITION

Canoes are one of the oldest universal tools used by humankind. The oldest archaeologically recovered canoe was discovered in the Netherlands and dates between 8200 – 7600 BC. Use of the canoe to facilitate transportation, food gathering, and communication made it one of the most important innovations for many cultures. Ancient canoes have been discovered around the world from frozen northern climates to steamy tropical lands. Countless more are undoubtedly still buried, waiting to be discovered, preserved, and interpreted.

By studying canoes, archaeologists can illuminate key elements of human behavior, such as subsistence methods, technologies, or distances traveled. One of the ways we understand the aquatic tradition of Mississippians is by depictions on artifacts. Four matching fragments of an engraved marine-shell cup from the Craig Mound, at Spiro, OK, depict four men in two canoes.

A great advantage for American archaeologists is that ca-

School Children discovered an ancient canoe around Arklow, Ireland in 1966. The National Museum dated the canoe to between Neolithic and Medieval period.

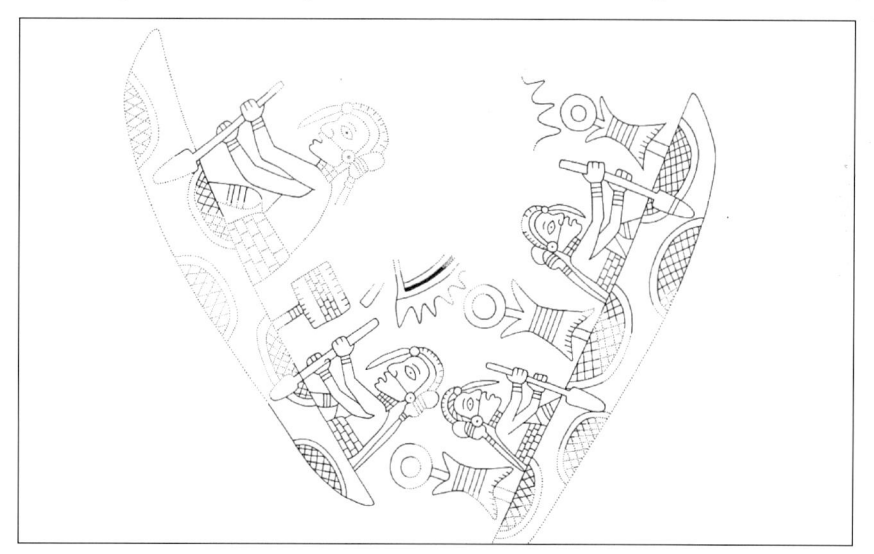

Plate 160 from Philip Phillips and James A. Brown, Pre-Columbian Shell Engravings from the Craig Mound at Spiro, Oklahoma, Paperback Edition Part 2. Peabody Museum Press. Copyright 1984 by the President and Fellows of Harvard College.

Frederick Kemmelmeyer painting Christopher Columbus. *It depicts the explorer's 1492 landing on San Salvador Island. It was completed around 1805 or 1806.*

in which different groups throughout North America adapted canoes for their needs. There was not a single type of mass-produced canoe for all North American Native Peoples, but rather a diversity of styles that reflected the multiplicity of native cultures, and the uniqueness of their environment.

Many Europeans kept journals detailing their first encounters with North America- its people, land, and wildlife. Captured in these accounts are details about the diversity, power, and beauty of canoes. One such surviving account is from Christopher Columbus and dated Saturday, October 13, 1492,

"They came to the ship in boats, which are made of a tree-trunk like a long boat and all of one piece. They are very wonderfully carved, considering the country, and large, so that in some, forty or forty-five men came. Others are smaller, so that in some only a solitary man came. They row them with a paddle, like a baker's peel, and they travel wonderfully fast. If one capsizes, all at once they begin to swim and right it, bailing it out with gourds which they carry with them."

Columbus's descriptive narrative highlights the diversity in style and function for canoes. Some canoes were artistically carved and embellished, while others fulfilled a more utilitarian role.

Another account comes to us from Spanish troops during their expeditions into Florida and North America's southeastern

noes, and artifacts depicting them, not only appear in the archaeological record, but written accounts of canoes appear in historic documents as well. Several surviving sources describe the variety of canoe sizes, shapes, materials, and uses, as well as methods

region. The Gentleman of Elvas, who recorded Hernando DeSoto's journey, wrote of a vast Native American fleet that approached them along the Mississippi River. This is his description of the war fleet of the chief Quigualtam in 1543.

"Then next day, the cacique [Spanish word for the leader of an indigenous group] came with two hundred canoes full of Indians with their bows, and arrows, painted with red ocher and having great plumes of white and many colored feathers on either side [of the canoes] and holding shields in their hands with which they covered the paddlers, while the warriors were standing from prow to stern with their bows and arrows in their hands. The canoe in which the cacique came had an awning spread in the stern and he [the cacique] was seated under a canopy. Also other canoes came bearing Indian notables. The chief [of each canoe] from his position under the canopy, controlled and gave orders to the men."

The Gentleman of Elvas continues, describing this scene along the Mississippi River, as Native forces descended on their position,

"Those canoes were very pleasing to see, for they were very large and well built; and together with the awnings, the plumes of feathers, the shields, and banners, and the many men in them, they had the appearance of a beautiful fleet of galleys."

The men on both Columbus and DeSoto's expeditions highly regarded the craftsmanship of the canoes. While the Spaniards found the canoes extremely efficient watercrafts, and beautiful works of art, the DeSoto expedition learned that they were also efficient instruments of warfare on the mighty Mississippi.

Theodore De Bry's sketch showing European and Natives trading. Completed c. 1634.

How Do We Know?

MUCH OF OUR VISUAL INFORMATION ABOUT NATIVE AMERICANS AT THE TIME of European contact comes from a few explorer/artists that traveled the continent. As they moved through North America they documented what they saw- the people, landscape, and wildlife. One of these explorer artists was John White. John was born in England around 1540 and first sailed to North America in 1585 landing in what is now North Carolina.

On this expedition, John served as mapmaker and artist. He was commissioned to "draw to life" the inhabitants of the New World so that their representations could be seen and studied back in England. During his time at Roanoke Island he created several watercolors that depict the landscape and Native Americans of the eastern coast. These are extremely important as they are the most informative illustrations of Native American life on the eastern seaboard at the time of European contact. This initial expedition was not successful and the men returned to England in 1586.

Portrait of John White- explorer, artist, and governor of Roanoke colony. White's original maps and sketches preserve aspects of Native American culture at the time of European arrival on the eastern coast of North America.

Dugouts

Preserved historical accounts recount how Native Americans made a variety of watercraft, from vast to small, and from decorated to utilitarian. Beyond size and function there are also varieties in shape and construction. While many variations exist, four varieties highlighted in this section are dugouts, rafts, skin boats, and bark boats.

Dugout canoes were the main source of water transportation for Mississippians, as well as other culture groups. Scholars have estimated that around 50% of Mississippian populations' protein intake was from fish and waterfowl. Shallow-drafted canoes would have greatly facilitated procuring the game as well as transporting catches back to the settlements. Ethnographic accounts describe nighttime fishing from dugout canoes. Night fishing was a frequent Mississippian practice. Fishermen would build a fire in clay basins and place it in the canoes. This would illuminate the river bottom and daze fish, making them easy targets for men with spears and nets. Dugouts were also used to place trotlines (heavy lines with baited hooks attached at intervals), and to collect fish from weirs and traps.

There is evidence of charring in the interior of the newly-acquired ancient canoe. This has been interpreted to be evidence of small controlled fires built in the bow. This shows that canoes were not just important to fishing just because they could transport the fisherman, but also because they provided tools that would help fishing productivity. This is also seen in the engraving by Theodore De Bry (1528-1598), which depicts Native Americans in Virginia fishing with a fire in the middle of their canoe.

In the background of the De Bry engraving you can see a fishing weir. A weir is an obstruction that partially or wholly covers a river or tidal waters and is constructed to direct fish into a trap. Native American weirs were constructed out of either woven wooden stakes or stones. Canoes were not only helpful in building weirs in the water, but also in gathering fish that had been caught in the weirs. Contact era historical accounts attest to weirs being used by eastern seaboard tribes. Europeans who expanded into the mid-continent did not describe Native Americans using weirs. But based on archaeological finds, which have been identified as weirs, we know that in fact they were used throughout the mid-continent.

Theodore De Bry engraving of Native Americans preparing fish. Fish were an important resource for Cahokians. After catching them using weirs, fishing lines, and nets they would have prepared them for consumption.

John White watercolor of Native Americans fishing with fire, and using spears and weirs.

The canoe displayed in our gallery exhibit is a prime example of a dugout. This type of canoe was constructed from a single wooden log. Tall and straight trees were needed for dugout construction. Bald cypress trees were the optimal variety for canoes. In other areas of the southeast, dugout canoes have been found made of pine and poplar. Like bald cypress, these trees have large straight sections and fewer knots than other varieties. While examples exist of archaeologically recovered canoes made from all three types of trees, the majority are constructed from bald cypress.

Historic photo showing a Nez Perce man in a dugout canoe. The Nez Perce live in the Pacific Northwest.

Bald cypress trees were prized for their notoriously straight trunks and rot resistant properties, both important qualities when fashioning a canoe. The trees are also recognizable due to their unique "knees" that grow above the waterline.

Bald Cypress *(Taxodium distichum)*

THE BALD CYPRESS SHARES ITS LONG LIST OF ATTRIBUTES WITH ONLY A HANDful of tree species. The wood is known for its water repellant and decay resistant properties, is very lightweight, and bald cypress wood has been a favorite of craftsmen and carpenters for at least 1,000 years. For these reasons, cypress wood has long been preferred in the construction of homes, fences, boats, river pilings, and greenhouses, to name a few. Some of the old-growth trees have been found to be very rot-resistant. It has been found that second-growth trees lack the decay resistant qualities of the old-growth trees.

Native to North America, it flourishes in humid environments, and is found primarily in the Southeastern United States and the Gulf Coast Plains. Inland, its range extends along the middle and upper coastal plain streams, through the Mississippi Valley, and into Missouri and southern Illinois. It mostly grows in flat, alluvial soils, at elevations of less than 50 meters above sea level and usually in wetlands. Stands are common in Louisiana, Florida, and parts of Texas, with some of the oldest stands growing in Florida. Recently, the bald cypress has become a popular landscape tree because the adaptations that allow it to flourish in wet, riverine conditions also allow it to flourish in the deeply compacted soils of urban landscapes. Its natural range has been extended because of this.

The most common method used to make a dugout was to light a small, carefully controlled fire on top of the log. As sections burned the builders would scrape away the charred areas with stone adzes, axes, gouges, or shells. Sometimes, wet clay was applied to areas not burned.

Theodore De Bry engraving based off a John White sketch entitled The Manner of Making their Boats, *1590. This image shows Native Americans using the burn and scrape method of dugout canoe construction.*

Adze and Axe

STONE ADZES ARE SIMILAR LOOKING TO AXES, BUT they have a flat as well as a convex side. The flat side of the adze head is strapped to a wooden handle. An adze blade runs perpendicular to the length of the handle, whereas an axe head runs parallel. The right angle of the head to the handle allows for a more "chipping" action rather than a "chopping" axe-like motion.

An adze and axe. Note the flat side of the adze that rests along wooden handle. This allows for the more chopping or pulling action needed to properly use an adze. Both sides of the axe were convex. Sketches courtesy of Bill Iseminger.

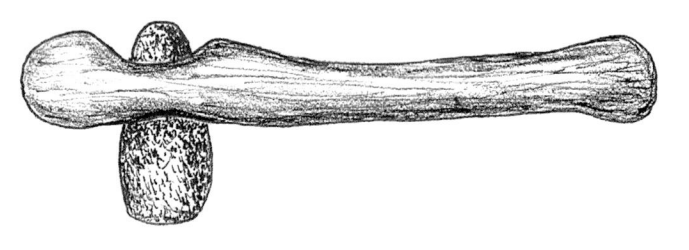

Without the use of fire, Native Americans would have found it nearly impossible to sculpt a canoe from a whole tree. It simply would have required too much time and energy to produce a single canoe. However, if fire was used along with their existing tool set, the speed of manufacturing increased dramatically. The exteriors of canoes were also shaped using stone and shell tools. Looking back into the historical records, a passage of Samuel de Champlain's is preserved recounting Natives along the Massachusetts coast making a dugout:

"Those who inhabit it have canoes all made in one piece, very easy to upset...After having taken much trouble and spent a long time in felling the largest and tallest tree that they can find with stone hatchets, they take off the bark and round it all but one side, where they set fires every little way all along the log. Sometimes they take red-hot pebbles, which they also put on it, and when the fire is too fierce they extinguish it with a little water, not entirely, but only enough to prevent the edge of the canoe from being burned. When it is as much hollowed out as they wish, they scrape it all over with stones."

The entire process was an intricate and lengthy one, relying on small, controlled fires that slowly burn away the log's interior. If steps changed, there could be drastic effects on the quality of the canoe. For example, if they burned the interior at a faster pace they risk burn-

Burning a section of a log in the burn and scrape method of canoe construction.

ing through the log or setting fire to the entire log. If they gave up on fire altogether and just chopped and scraped at the interior there is the risk of splitting or damaging the integrity of the log.

You can still see the individual tool marks and some charring along the interior of the canoe now on display in the Interpretive Center. While the size of canoes could vary greatly, dugouts were generally long and narrow, with thin walls and straight sides.

They often had platforms at both ends and sometime a hole in one platform, probably for mooring.

Based on ethnographic, historical, and archaeological research we know that Native Americans made dugout canoes in a wide variety of forms. The size and shape of dugouts was dictated by the intended purpose and the environment it was to traverse.

Boats that had a flat-bottom with more square-shaped ends were used to navigate shallow waters. A late nineteenth century account describes this type of boat looking somewhat like a narrow rowboat. This type would have been most suitable for local travel, perhaps navigating a lake or small river system. These boats would not have been used to carry large loads of goods or many passengers.

Another type of canoe had a narrow middle with sharper and taller ends. It is the most commonly recognized dugout canoe shape. Often the canoe is just wide enough to allow people to sit and usually ranges in length between 11-30 feet. The gunwales and interior are finished to a smoothed surface, and the bow and stern are shaped so there is a visible difference between them.

This most common style can be further altered with an extended and overhanging bow. The shape of the rest of the canoe remains the same but the modified bow shape allows the watercraft to negotiate rougher waters. The new bow would have allowed the canoe to adapt to swift currents and breaking waves. These boats would have been useful on larger lakes and faster rivers. Specific elements of design, such as those present on this type of canoe, helped alleviate the effort needed to make it across to the other shore.

Another dugout canoe style resembled barge and load carrying ships. These had a wide bottom and a wide bow and stern, making the boat much more stable in order to carry heavy loads over shallow waters. These types of boats would have been crucial for moving goods and food. Having canoes that were able to handle large loads, along with the vast connected waterways meant that goods were able to travel far distances and at much greater speeds than by carrying them over land.

Stepping up in size, the next type was catamaran-like canoes. A catamaran vessel is one that has multiple hulls that are connected to ensure stability. A major benefit of this multi-hulled canoe is that it is lighter, allowing the canoe to have a shallow draught. This reduces drag and allows the vessel to reach faster speeds. The two hulls are joined by some structure. There is archaeological evidence for two catamaran canoes in the Southeast. Both excavated canoes have carved or drilled holes along the top edge of the gunwales, which is most likely where the central support was connected.

Theodore De Bry

THEODORE DE BRY WAS AN ENGRAVER WHO DOCUMENTED VISUAL information about Native American culture at the time of European contact. Men like John White would paint watercolors depicting the people and landscapes. Then these watercolors would be transformed into engraved illustrations by a prestigious engraver, such as De Bry, back in Europe. De Bry was born in Belgium and later moved to Strasburg, Antwerp, London, and Frankfurt. He is most famous for his works known as "The Discovery of America." De Bry himself never traveled across the Atlantic, which shows in the European attributes he gives Native American subjects in his engravings. Beyond appearances, he also took liberties by depicting scenes of cannibalism and mixing tribal customs and artifacts. His works were published in Latin, but then translated into German, English, and French allowing them to reach an even greater public. De Bry was fundamental to how 16th-century Europeans conceived of North America and the native people who inhabited it.

Theodore De Bry's Human Cannibalism *was a fictitious engraving. De Bry took many liberties in his portrayal of Native Americans, and his images reached many Europeans and increased misinformation about the inhabitants of North America.*

John Webber's Hawaiian Navigators Sailing Multi-Hulled Canoe, 1781. Webber was an artist on Captain Cook's ship. These catamaran, multi-hulled canoes reduce drag and increase speed of the canoe.

In addition to archaeological evidence, historical accounts tell of two boats that were joined together. One such excerpt from Menendez and Dickinson (Purdy 1991) states that, "the Calusa chief Carlos came with as many as 12 canoes and two of them fastened one to the other, with decks covered with awnings of hoops and matting." Included with catamaran vessels are those that have been cut in half, length wise, and widened by the addition of a central plank. This practice increases the width of the bed allowing the canoe to hold more goods or passengers. The joints are sealed with either cleats or wooden pegs.

Rafts, Bull Boats, and Bark Canoes

Many floating objects are often considered rafts. The difference between a buoyant log and a raft is that rafts are typically flat or "platform-shaped." They are considered the most basic boat design because they do not have hulls. Rafts are kept afloat by using lightweight and buoyant construction materials like wood, sticks, or branches, which are lashed together. Wood is lighter than water and allows the raft to float even when fully loaded. Rafts were useful for river crossings, but not for long distance travel.

Bull boats, or skin boats, are bowl-shaped vessels that use animal hides as a primary fabrication component. The boats are supported by a wood or bone framework and encased in animal skins. Due to this unique fabrication method they are often referred to as skin boats. These boats were predominantly used in northern plains. Skin boats are relatively light and can be easily taken apart and carried over land until needed again. These boats are an effective method of water transportation in areas where materials, such as large trees, are scarce.

Karl Bodmer's watercolor Mandan Bull Boats, *1832. This painting shows women of the Mandan tribe using bull boats to cross a river. The Mandan historically lived along the Missouri River in present-day North and South Dakota.*

a winter thaw. A cut is made down the length of the tree with two cuts circling the top and bottom. The bark is then peeled from the tree in a single sheet. Removing the bark does not kill the tree. It will heal and grow a new outer layer of bark. An interior wooden frame was used to ensure the stability and shape of the canoe. The bark strips would wrap around the frame with their ends stitched together and sealed with gum or pitch (pitch is a sticky substance

A subset variety of bull boats were buffalo boats, primarily used by Plains tribes to transport goods by river. They used the same bowl-shaped wooden frame covered in buffalo skin (the hairy side faces outwards). They looked like a large hairy bowl but, despite their more unique appearance, they could carry up to a half-ton of cargo. However, their round shape made them slower and more difficult to steer than traditionally shaped canoes. Another interesting fact about bull boats is that they were usually made and paddled by women.

Bark canoes are aptly named as they are made from a wide strips of tree bark. Birch or elm are best for this style of construction. The bark is removed from the trees in early spring or during

Shooting the Rapids, *by Frances Anne Hopkins, depicts French voyageurs in a large bark canoe maneuvering their way around rapids in a large river. Europeans readily adopted the canoe technology of Native Americans as they moved westward through North America.*

made from sap, fat, and charcoal). Bark canoes are very light, making them easy to transport over ground if necessary. Even though they were susceptible to damage by rocks, bark canoes were able to transport heavy loads in shallow waters.

Residents of the Great Lakes or upper Northeast region probably consider bark canoes synonymous with Native Americans. While they certainly are the most prevalent type in those regions, the trees that produce the correct type of bark do not grow throughout the country. Also bark was not always a durable enough material to handle rough waters. In other areas of North America, indigenous groups had to use other materials to make efficient watercraft.

The bark canoes favored by tribes from these more northern regions were ill-suited for large interior river systems of the mid-continent and southeast. Bark canoes are highly maneuverable and light enough to be carried over ground. However, they were too fragile against the ice, flotsam, and sometimes even large fish that were found throughout large rivers. Europeans traveling the mid-continent soon copied the Native Peoples, who used sturdy dugout canoes to maneuver the extensive river systems.

CONNECTED WATERWAYS

While the Mississippi River visually and geographically dominates the midcontinent, there are thousands of small streams, backwater lakes, tributaries, and swamps that together form a system of interconnected waterways. This extensive aquatic system gave Cahokians access to lands and environments on both local and regional scales. Cahokians capitalized on the abundance of water and cultural knowledge of canoe construction. The relationship between humans and their surroundings is best captured by Mikko Saikku in his work *This Delta, This Land*,

"Environmental factors have to be included among key elements when historical explanations are constructed. Environmental conditions set the ultimate boundaries for human societies and their activities."

Early historical accounts of Native Americans describe them as great navigators. During the years of European expansion and subjugation of Native Americans, that characteristic of their cultures was repressed. More recently scholars have reemphasized this skill and, as one historian states it, "…the prowess of the American Indian as a navigator has been greatly underestimated…The Mississippi, with its tributaries, constituted an extensive river highway in a country of forests. The towns built beside it show in their cultural similarity that the river was heavily travelled."

◀ Map of American Bottom circa 1800 with locations of mound groups. Courtesy of Powell Archaeology, Mikels Skele, Archaeology Laboratory, Southern Illinois University at Edwardsville.

Floodplain Formation and Geography

The Mississippian city of Cahokia is located in the heart of the American Bottom, a term given to the 175-square mile Mississippi floodplain. It stretches from Alton, Illinois in the north, down a hundred miles to near Chester, Illinois in the south. The American Bottom is named for the influx of American settlers after the Revolutionary War in order to distinguish it from the Spanish owned territory west of the Mississippi. This area provides a wide variety of flora and fauna in a condensed space, near the confluence of major waterways. This made the American Bottom a truly unique environment for the development of a complex society.

The duration of Late Woodland and Mississippian settlement at Cahokia in the American Bottom spans at most 500 years, a relative moment in the floodplain's history. The floodplain's beginnings stretch back 540 million years ago to the Paleozoic Era when the underlying bedrock was formed as an ancient seabed. During the Pleistocene Epoch (also known as the Ice Age), the floodplain was built up with glacial outwash sediment deposition occurring over thousands of millennia (2.5 million to 11,500 years ago). The final development occurred during the Holocene (11,500 years ago to present) with repetitive erosion and deposition of sediment by the meandering Mississippi River. Floodplains and their associated rivers are always in a dynamic balance between the accumulation and removal of sediment. The sediment (or alluvial fill) varies throughout the American Bottom from 0 to 160 feet deep. Today the mighty Mississippi is controlled by a system of levees and monitored by teams of engineers. But just over 100 years ago, the river was an unconstrained tempest- seasonally swelling, wandering across the open floodplain, carving and shaping with the power of her waters. The American Bottom preserves evidence of thousands of years of river movement with meander scars, terraces, oxbow lakes, ridges, and many other scattered landforms.

The Mississippi River geologically dominates the mid-continent. As the fourth longest river in the world, it is not only an environmental feature in itself, but also acts as the drainage system for the world's fourth largest watershed that covers 40% of the lower 48 states. This resulted in an expansive network of interconnected waterways and Cahokia was in the perfect location to exploit and, later, dominate it. The American Bottom floodplain with its backwater lakes and slow streams provided resources and transportation in the immediate area.

The river travels 2,340 miles from its origins in Lake Itasca, Minnesota, down to the Gulf of Mexico. Before the river reaches St.

Geomorphic Glossary:

Slough: Sunken hollows or channels adjacent to the river, possibly filled with slow-moving water.

Swale: Low tracts of land between ridges that are often marshy. These low areas can hold stagnant water depending on the season.

Terrace: Flat step-like landforms that are most frequently found along bluffs and floodplain edges.

Point Bar: When sediment is deposited along the inner bend of a river.

Cut Bank: Formed along the outside banks of rivers; these sides of the channel continually undergo erosion and are often shaped like small cliffs.

Alluvial Fan: Fan or cone-shaped deposits created by moving water, usually where rivers exit the uplands and spill onto the floodplain.

Oxbow Lake: As a river shifts course and the meander is cut off from the main channel, the meander forms a "U-shaped" body of water, called an oxbow lake.

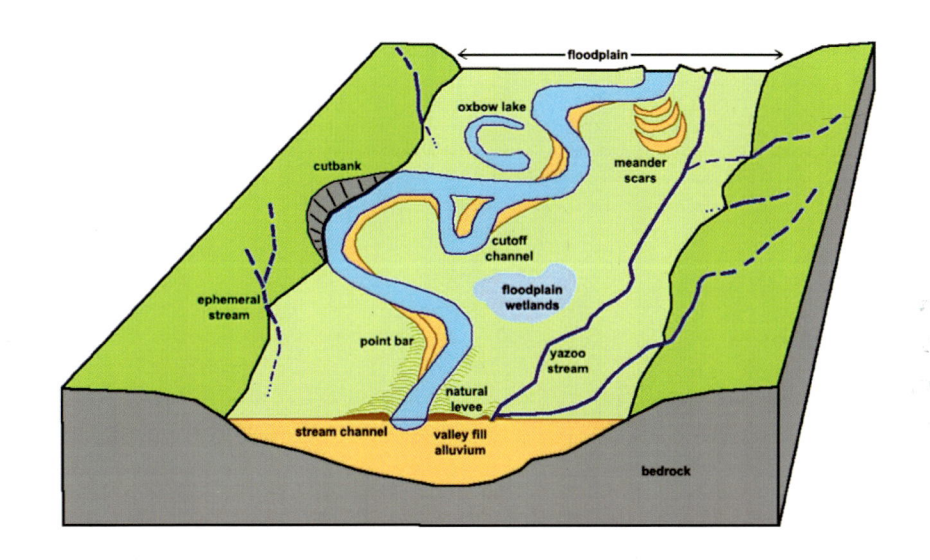

This floodplain cutaway illustrates different geomorphic features typically found on a flat floodplain. The diversity of features creates a variety of habitats for plants and animals.

Cutoff Channel: Formed when a river finds a new and shorter path by "cutting off" the neck of a meander. This process isolates the oxbow lake while also giving the river a shorter course.

Natural Levee: Long ridges of mud or silt that build up adjacent to the banks of a floodplain stream, usually higher on the outer cut-bank side.

Louis, Missouri, it cuts deeply into the Paleozoic bedrock creating a defined valley. This section of the river is known as the Upper Mississippi. The Middle Mississippi section begins at the confluence with the Missouri River, just north of St. Louis. This meeting of two rivers also reflects substantial changes in the nature of the river's course.

Below the confluence of the Mississippi and Missouri, the floodplain widens (the American Bottom) and the Mississippi takes a meandering pattern. The Missouri River contributes a significant amount of water and sediment to the Mississippi, increasing its flow by almost 50 percent. The Missouri maintains an average gradient of 1 foot per mile (around twice as steep at the Mississippi) so it is able to carry coarser river bottom sand and gravel. This results in the distinct change in the Mississippi's color as the river passes the confluence. Another river, the Illinois, joins the Mississippi just north of where the Missouri enters. South of these two confluences the Mississippi combines features of all three rivers. The Mississippi is not only susceptible to fluctuation from local events, such as dry or wet years, but also from climactic changes as far away as each tributaries' origins.

The Middle Mississippi section continues until the confluence of the Ohio River, where the floodplain widens even more (up to 50 miles!). Past the Ohio River the Lower Mississippi meanders its way back and forth down to the Gulf of Mexico. It enters the Gulf at a rate between 200 and 700 cubic feet per second.

Today one can travel from Minneapolis to St. Louis by air, drive there via highways, or take a train or bus. But for Mississip-

Map of the Mississippi River and its main tributaries. The outlined area represents the Mississippi's watershed, which covers approximately 40% of the continental United States.

pians living 800 years ago there were only two choices– canoe on the Mississippi River, or walk. Native Americans did not have pack animals or beasts of burden. Horses, which pop culture so closely associates with western Native Americans, were only re-introduced to the continent after Spanish arrival, around AD 1519. Anything Mississippians needed to bring with them, they had to carry. This made water transportation much more efficient

Historic photo of two Native Caribs transporting goods by dugout canoe. Water transportation allows for people to move more and heavier items than by land.

in terms of time as well as energy spent for moving goods. Many studies have been conducted on the efficiency of water versus land transportation. When it comes to moving goods via water, it can take less than half the time needed for land transportation and up to 450% more cargo can be moved with the same amount of energy expended. If four people are traveling 50 miles on water, they would save 25,000 calories compared to the same group moving over land. However, for water transportation there is a natural limit of water and where it travels on the landscape.

Trade

Archaeologists are able to trace the extent of Mississippian trade by examining patterns in the archaeological record. Just like our culture today, objects and styles went in and out of fashion for Mississippians. Different pottery styles are representative of certain times. The same applies to varieties of ceremonial or engraved objects. If archaeologists uncover these types of objects in the same context as a midden (trash deposits), house, or mound, they can then date the construction of those features to the same time as that pottery style. In addition to stratigraphy (the concept that items found lower in the ground are usually older than those found above) dating of artifact styles is one of the older methods of establishing chronology for archaeologists.

For Mississippians, canoes not only facilitated long-distance trade for material objects but also for the exchange of ideas. For example, let's look at three different Cahokian-styled objects: Ramey Incised Pottery, Cahokia Flintclay Figurines, and Long-Nosed God Ear Ornaments.

Ramey Incised Pottery: Ramey Incised pottery was a Mississippian ceramic tradition, highly used throughout Cahokia and the American Bottom. The presence of these ceramics outside the floodplain region points to their use as containers for exchanged goods. There are several styles and designs associated with Ramey pottery, each with its own unique symbolic meaning.

Cahokia Flintclay Figurines: Although called "pipestone," flintclay is actually a soft sedimentary rock. Archaeologists have traced this Cahokian variety of flintclay to local sources in the Cahokia region and it is believed most pipes and figurines made from this material were actually made at or near Cahokia. Of interesting note is the spatial distribution of different gendered figurines. Archaeologists more commonly find male figurines farther away from Cahokia, while they unearth female figurines closer to the city.

Long-Nosed God Ear Ornaments: These ear adornments represent a supernatural being, depicted with a small shield-shaped

Ramey Incised Pot.

Flintclay Figurine.

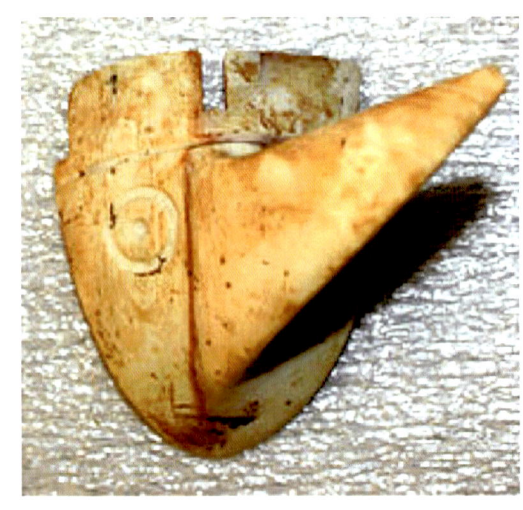

Long-Nosed God Ear Ornament, made of shell.

face and a large nose of various lengths. The ornaments were made of shell, copper, or bone. Men wore these ornaments suspended from their ears in imitation of the supernatural being, He-Who-Wears-Human-Heads-As-Earrings.

Cahokians traded these three artifact types as well as many other items with Mississippian settlements throughout the mid-continent. Canoes and the interconnected waterways were the mechanisms of trade and transportation that allowed these items to move between settlements. This map illustrates the distribution pattern for the three previously described artifact types over the mid-continent. Clusters center around major rivers, such as the Mississippi, Illinois, Missouri, Tennessee, Arkansas, and Red Rivers. The system of waterways allowed these items to be traded as far north as Minnesota and as far south as Louisiana.

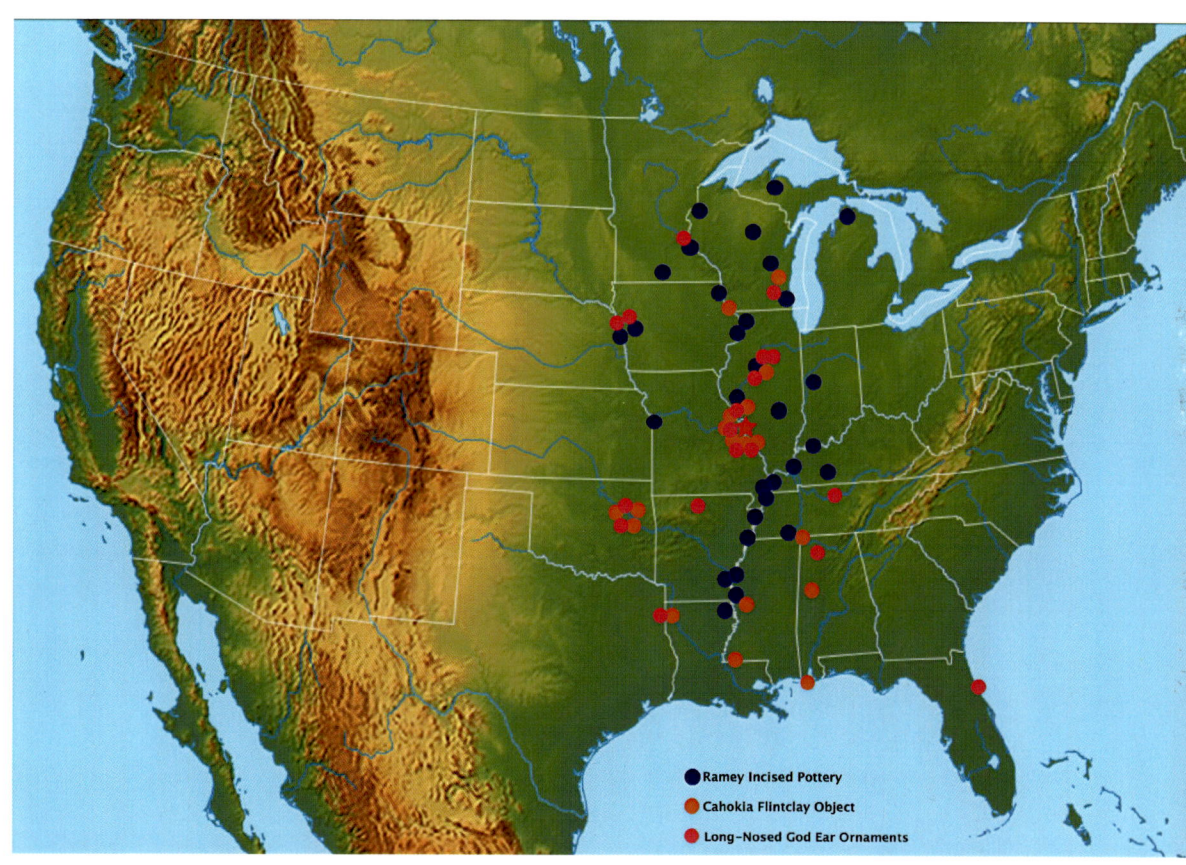

This map shows where objects from these three categories (Ramey Incised Pottery, Cahokia Flintclay Object, and Long-Nosed God Ear Ornaments) were discovered. Map courtesy of Tim Pauketat. Red star denotes Cahokia.

Ceremonial Expression and Exchange

Archaeologists are able to trace extents of trade patterns by examining the distribution of Cahokian-styled objects. But how do archaeologists know what constitutes a Cahokia-made item? While many daily items were traded: pottery, hides, meat, seeds, etc., other types of more ritually significant or ceremonial objects were also exchanged between groups and communities. Certain designs on ceremonial art also seem to indicate a direct or at least ideological connection to Cahokia. These "icons" appear somewhat consistently in ceremonial context throughout the Southeast and have been referred to as the Southeastern Ceremonial Complex (SECC).

While some scholars debate its title and appropriateness due to concerns over large-scale interpretation and a catch-all mentality, the SECC most likely indicates not only trade connections between Cahokia and other Mississippian settlements, but also reflects an exchange or sharing of belief systems. Archaeologists have traced two major SECC styles over time and space. The most ubiquitous and influential was Classic Braden style. It is believed that Cahokia was largely responsible for the development and proliferation of this style. Its figurative subject matter has precursors in the Midwestern prairies and forests. The symbols, stories, and supernatural beings did not just appear with Cahokia, but were derived from previous regional groups. Themes and motifs that exemplify the Braden style are exemplified in the famous Rogan Plates.

These two copper embossed plates were discovered at Etowah Mounds in Georgia in the 1880s. It is currently theorized that the plates were manufactured at or near Cahokia and later transported to Etowah. The plates depict characters that exhibit anthropomorphic and zoomorphic characteristics. One recognizable character is that of Birdman, also known as Hawk. This theme is very common throughout SECC imagery and depicts a very important supernatural being for Mississippian cosmological beliefs.

In addition to material trade objects, cosmological beliefs, both their understanding and thematic artistic representation,

This shell gorget, discovered in Castilian Springs Tennessee, depicts a warrior in imitation of Morning Star. In his hands he holds the severed head of his enemy as well as ceremonial mace. He also is depicted with a forked eye motif and a bi-lobed arrow headdress. These are all common motifs in the Classic Braden style.

One of the Rogan Plates, which are a set of copper plates discovered at the Etowah site. In keeping with Classic Braden style the figure is depicted with a forked eye, bi-lobed arrow headdress, as well as the avian characteristics of the Morning Star supernatural being.

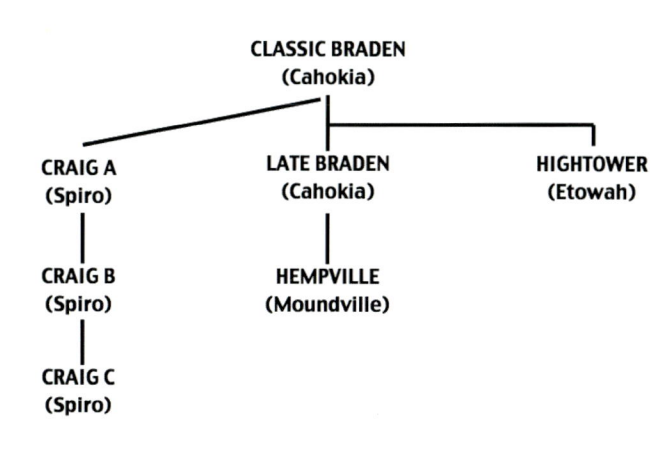

The diagram illustrates the spread and adaptation of Southeastern Ceremonial Complex styles. They all grew from the Classic Braden style, which originated at Cahokia.

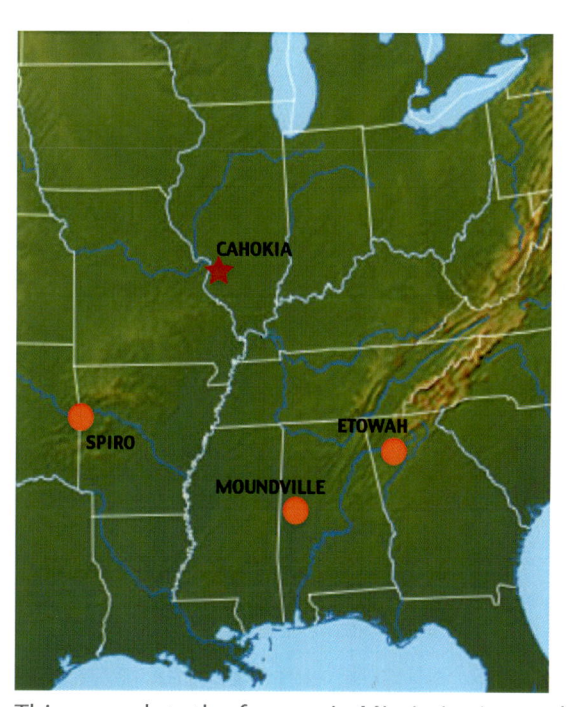

This map plots the four main Mississippian and Southeastern Ceremonial Complex cities. This represents the hub of Mississippian culture.

were also traded and transported around the Mississippian world. Archaeologists have used radiocarbon dates to trace this stylistic transformation and expansion from Cahokia to other settlements. The current model of development is as follows.

Three other large Mississippian settlements adopted the Classic Braden style. These were Spiro, in Oklahoma, Moundville in Alabama, and Etowah in Georgia.

This map below shows their location in relation to Cahokia. In order for these settlements to have similar iconography and ceremonial objects, like the Rogan Plates, ideas and objects had to move over great distances, and the interconnected waterways of the Mississippi River and its tributaries were key in facilitating this ideological and material exchange.

Raw Material Trade

There was also extensive trade in raw materials that were used for daily or common purposes. Often attention is paid to the ceremonial or exotic trade goods because of the allure of their beauty and uniqueness. These are considered elite goods, and help us to understand social complexity and how elites influenced exchange networks. It is often the utilitarian items that better illustrate the extent and intricacy of Native American trade networks. These objects were more frequent and circulated through more settlements, providing a bigger picture of relationships and trade patterns between communities.

The American Bottom is located between several distinct regional ecosystems with diverse raw materials. Mississippian communities around the Middle Mississippi area sought out raw materials from these various regions for their own use and for trade opportunities. To the southwest of the American Bottom is the Ozark region. It consists of a higher plateau that expands throughout lower Missouri, into Arkansas and Oklahoma. This region's bedrock formation created a unique environment with a variety of raw materials. Mississippians gathered salt, galena (lead ore), hematite (iron ore), flintclay, chert, basalt, granite, and other igneous rocks. Chert was chipped into tools and weapons and igneous rocks were pecked and ground to make axes and other tools, as well as ritual objects. Eighty percent of the chert found at Cahokia is Burlington chert from the Ozark foothills south and west of St. Louis. Flintclay was used to make the beautiful figurines discussed above.

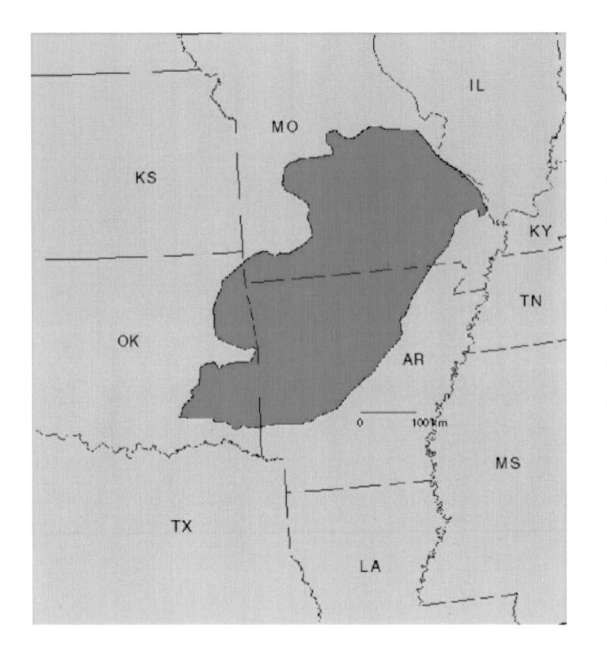

The dark area marks the area of the Ozarks. They begin just to the south of St. Louis, Missouri and extend into Arkansas and the eastern edge of Oklahoma.

Salt was produced from springs in the Ozarks as well. The Native people harvested salt by boiling water from the springs until the water evaporated. All that remained was salt. One of these salt production resources was located near a fortified Mississippian town. While there was an increase in warfare, or at least a threat of it (e.g., the stockade walls at Cahokia) during the Mississippian period, it is interesting that a community located very near a raw material was fortified. Salt being such a desired commodity, this community may have felt the need to fortify their location against possible attacks from others claiming ownership or the right to access the same resource. These raw materials that originate in the Ozarks are found throughout the mid-continent. Cahokians appear to be the biggest consumers of Ozark materials. It is also possible that Cahokia may have been responsible for redistributing these resources throughout the greater area.

There are also many varieties of chert and stone that were traded during Mississippian times. Two of the more widely known varieties are Mill Creek Chert and Hixton Silicified Sandstone. The Mill Creek quarry was located in southern Illinois, down the Mississippi, about 125 miles south of Cahokia. Hixton was in west central Wisconsin, 465 miles north of Cahokia. Compared to food and other perishable materials, it is easier for archaeologists to note trade patterns from the distribution of chert and stone objects.

This shows the source locations for important natural resources for the Cahokians. The Ozarks are rich in salt, galena, hematite, and flintclay. Also noted are the locations of Hixton Silicified Sandstone and Mill Creek Chert.

A crane stands in the shallow water at the edge of a lake near Cahokia.
Photo courtesy of Bob Ahrens.

AMERICAN BOTTOM RESOURCES

The dynamic nature of the Mississippi River shaped the surrounding land for thousands of years. Before modern levees and modifications, the river routinely flooded, depositing sediments, replenishing soils throughout the floodplains. The natural system of backwater lakes, wetlands, and swales would have helped absorb excess floodwaters. The cyclical rising and falling of the river brought rich life to the adjacent floodplain. These teeming backwaters supported a diverse bounty of aquatic, terrestrial, and avian life.

Scholars have noted up to fourteen distinct habitat zones in the American Bottom. An elevation change of a few inches can be the difference in submerged or dry soils and aquatic or terrestrial communities. A particular assemblage of plants, animals, soils, and topographic features defines each of the separate fourteen zones. The diversity of zones increased the natural resource capacity in the American Bottom. Therefore the American Bottom was equipped to support a varied and rich subsistence strategy for Native Americans.

Floodplain Environments

Over the last 10,000 years, the river's slow movement carried and deposited loose silt, sand, and clay forming the ridges, swales, and point bar deposits that shape the floodplain. The land resting between these undulating points was often covered, permanently or seasonally, in water. The American Bottom's backwaters consisted of creeks, lakes, wetlands, sloughs, and streams.

Photo of wetlands. Note the Bottomland forest off in the background and the mixture of water, plants, and animals.

Fish were a reliable and seasonally abundant resource and were an essential part of Cahokia's subsistence. Based on archaeologically recovered bones at the site, we know that fish were a significant and heavily exploited food source. Catfish from the Mississippi often grow as large as forty to sixty pounds, making them an ideal source of food for communal feasting. All the different water habitats, such as the Mississippi's main channel, slow moving creeks, oxbow lakes, and sluggish swamps, supported a diversity of species. These backwaters were inundated with water and reached their highest levels during the spring melt and rains, which corresponds to fish spawning season. Higher water levels allowed for a greater numbers of new fish, increasing the abundance in the backwaters. During the drier summer and early fall months, these shallow backwaters would shrink, trapping fish in isolated pools. This provided an excellent opportunity for Cahokians to catch the trapped fish with relative ease. Catfish and bullheads are the most commonly archaeologically recovered species. Also found are suckers, bass, sunfish, bowfin, gar, drum, and sturgeon.

Other groups of animals found in aquatic habitats include amphibians, mollusks, and reptiles. Commonly found are gray tree frogs, bullfrogs, American toads, and a number of freshwater mussels. While the mussels were used for food, their shells were also used to make tools and temper. Mussel shells were repurposed

Photo of a blue catfish. It's native distribution includes the Mississippi River and its drainage system.

Photo of a sucker fish. Suckers prefer deep fast waters and are often found in the main river channel.

Photo of a gar fish. The species is easily identifiable due to its long nose.

Photo of a mussel shell hoe.

Map of the Mississippi Flyway and migratory route for birds. Each spring and fall birds pass along the flyway on their way to and from Canada and South America. Photo courtesy of Texas Department of Parks and Wildlife.

for shell hoes, spoons, and ground up for tempering in ceramics. Box, snapping, and painted are the most common turtle varieties found in aquatic habitats. Turtle shells were modified into rattles that had ceremonial importance to Mississippian people. Their shells were also used for bowls, spoons, and cups.

Animals common in the wetlands are not limited to those that live in the water. Varieties of waterfowl lived throughout the American Bottom. Birds were not exploited to the same extent as fish and mammals, although they are continuously found in the archaeological record at Cahokia. The American Bottom's location along the Mississippi Flyway increased avian diversity and numbers. The flyway is an avian migration route that stretches from the Mackenzie River in Canada all the way down to the Gulf of Mexico and even into South America. Along the Mississippi, the floodplains, wetlands, forests, and grasslands provide food and shelter for the migrating birds. The American Bottom is just one small part of this enormous ecosystem, but its prime location along the flyway meant that Cahokians had access to a seasonal abundance and variety of birds. Geese, ducks, swans, cormorants, grebes, loons, coots, and rails are species that have been found archaeologically.

Also present, but to a lesser extent, are terrestrial birds. These include turkey, prairie chicken, grouse, and bobwhite. But when the number of turkey and other terrestrial avian bones are compared to those from migratory birds, the terrestrial species are a small percentage of all identifiable avian species in the total archaeological record.

Bottomland forests and prairies blanketed the areas that were not inundated with water. Forests often covered low and wet ground, along the banks of creeks and sloughs. These trees had to be water-tolerant and would grow wherever they were able to gain a permanent foothold. The two most common species of riparian trees were willows and cottonwoods. Further from the waters' edge other tree species formed dense wooded groves. These included pin oak, elm, poplar, locust, persimmon, ash, sycamore, hackberry, maple, and mulberry. These trees prefer a moist soil, and while they colonize higher and drier areas, there was always the potential for submergence. These trees provided timber and fuel for Cahokia's large population. Archaeologists have conducted charcoal analysis and discovered that much of the wood used as fuel in the Mississippian period was from hickory and oak trees. Cottonwoods and willows were predominately used for building structures.

Besides needing wood to construct buildings and for fuel, the most demanding project was the succession of stockade walls.

Image of Bottomland Forest.

Each version, at two miles long, of the wall required between 15,000-20,000 logs. Therefore a combined total of 60,000-80,000 logs were needed to build all four walls. Not every tree would have been a suitable size and shape. Logs were around a foot in diameter and had to be at least 20 feet tall. White oaks and hickories were found more on bluff slopes and bluff tops and where probably preferred for stockade construction. Stockade construction placed extreme pressure on timber sources and would have affected the amount of wooded area around the city, as well as the availability of plants and animals that lived in those bottomland forests.

Mature trees also provided an opportunity for Cahokians to collect nuts. Thick-shelled hickories are the most abundant nuts in archaeological contexts. Other varieties include pecans, black walnuts, butternuts, chestnuts, hazelnuts, and acorns. While differences in shell thickness and processing techniques could affect preservation there is still a clear emphasis on hickories. From Late Woodland to Mississippian times the proportions of nutshells do not greatly change. There is a slight increase in pecans and hazelnuts during the Mississippian period. This could indicate more localized gathering or possibly they had cut down many hickory trees for construction and they were less available. If the increasing population put more pressure on food resources, people might have had to supplement what was available with whatever was close at hand, including less preferred nuts.

Hickory trees were common in the American Bottom. They not only provided nuts as an additional food source, but also timber for construction and fuel.

Photo of hickory nuts.

Red Cedar *(Juniperus virginiana)*

OF ALL THE VARIETIES OF TREES AVAILABLE IN THE AMERICAN BOTTOM, RED cedar is one of the most common archaeologically recovered types. Cahokians restricted Red cedar for ceremonial purposes. It was burned so that its purifying smoke or incense could cleanse the body, soul, and sacred precincts. Its boughs were used in ceremonial rituals and structures to ward off evil powers. The red color of the wood led to its associations with fire and blood. The tree was also connected with water and life because of its "ever-lasting" (evergreen) qualities. Red cedar is also a naturally rot-resistant tree. Mature trees were used as the posts for Woodhenge, where the poles acted as a mediator between earth and sky during important astronomical and ritual ceremonies.

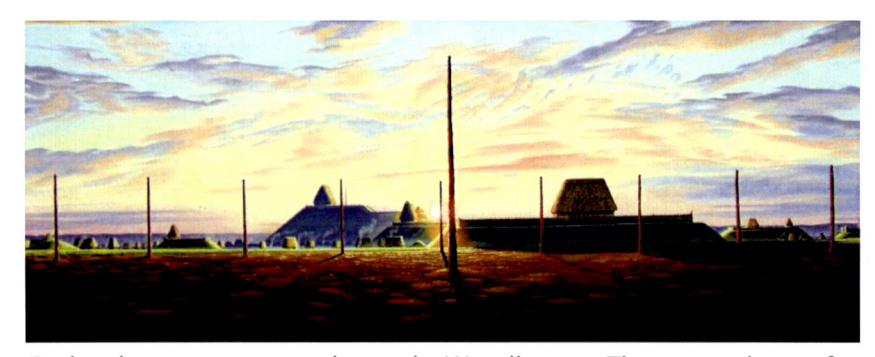

Red cedar trees were used to make Woodhenge. They were chosen for their unique coloring and rot resistant qualities. Red cedar was reserved for important ceremonial purposes. Painting by Bryan Haynes.

A thick-brushy undergrowth developed among the trees. While these plants grew in non-aquatic soils, they could survive periodic submergence and preferred damp soils to drier locations. Many of these plants were important to Cahokians for their medicinal properties and as food resources. Some important wild foods that grew in bottomland forests were wild cherries, grapes, blackberries, persimmons, pawpaws, and plums. These plants were gathered when ripe and supplemented their predominately crop based diet. These plants would have provided additional nutrients not found in game animals or crops, but wild fruits would have only held a secondary role in the general subsistence strategy for Cahokia. More often these wooded plants were selected for their potency and medicinal properties.

Prairies of varying sizes were scattered throughout the American Bottom. Because some prairies were better drained than others, the plant life that thrived in each patch was unique to the location. Early travelers to the

Photo of the Emiquon prairie on a foggy morning. Emiquon is located near Dickson Mounds in central Illinois.

area considered the prairies' richness quite extraordinary. In 1841 painter and lithographer Wild writes, "wide prairie stretches for miles its carpeting of green, gemmed with the most beautiful flowers, and dotted, at intervals, with clusters of trees."

Many small mammals found the brushy and grass filled prairies

Jack-in-the-Pulpit *(Arisaema triphyllum)*

A MEDICINAL PLANT COMMON THROUGHOUT BOTTOMLAND FORESTS WAS JACK-IN-the-pulpit. It can also be known as Indian Turnip or Memory-Root. The most identifiable characteristic of jack-in-the-pulpit is its cluster of bright red berries. The cup-like spathe is striped with dark and light green strips and typically curls over the spadix, giving the plant its unique appearance and is how it derived its name, as it resembles a man standing in a pulpit. The plant thrives in wet woods, swamps, or marsh environments.

Jack-in-the-pulpit contains calcium oxalate crystals. These crystals are poisonous when eaten and they can cause burning, irritation, and swelling if the plant is not properly prepared. However, these crystals that make jack-in-the-pulpit dangerous are also what gives the plant its medicinal qualities. In order to turn the potentially hazardous plant into a useful remedy, one must properly dry or cook parts of the plant. For example, the corms (underground growths, kind of like an onion) could be dried, pulverized, and applied as a counter irritant for rheumatism and pain. If the powdered corm was mixed with water and consumed, it acted as a contraceptive for women. One dose would prevent conception for a week. Two doses would induce permanent sterility.

Jack-in-the-pulpit had many different uses for Native Americans. The plant is recognizable for its cluster of red berries as well as its unique leaf structure that resembles a pulpit, hence its name.

perfect habitats. Small rodents, rabbits, raccoons, opossums, foxes, and gray squirrels thrived in prairies. Most likely, small-sized mammals were killed while Cahokians were engaged in other activities, such as fishing, tending crops, or gathering. Children could even have set traps for small animals. Men organized large hunts at times when no other pressing need demanded their labor. However, they would have been able to hunt smaller animals while performing other tasks if the opportunities presented themselves. While small mammals helped supplement Cahokians' diet, the percentage they provided was minimal compared to that of other animals.

Although small prairie mammals were not a major component of Cahokian diet they were still considered valuable animals. We know this because of the several legends and stories from modern tribes that featured prairie animals. Below is a story taken from the Omaha tribe. While the stories and words of Cahokians do not survive we can look to tribes who likely had connections with Cahokia and who may have accepted Cahokian citizens into their tribes after the depopulation of the city. This Omaha myth tells the story of How Rabbit Killed the Giant.

How Rabbit Killed the Giant (Omaha)

WHEN RABBIT WAS GOING ON A JOURNEY, HE CAME to a certain village. The people said, "Hello! Rabbit has come as a visitor." On meeting him, they said, "Whom did you come to see?"

"Why, I will go to the lodge of anyone," said Rabbit.

"But the people have nothing to eat," they said. "The Giant is the only one who has anything to eat. You ought to go to his lodge." Yet, the Rabbit passed on to the end lodge and entered it.

"Friend, we have nothing to eat," said the host.

"Why, my friend," said Rabbit, "when there is nothing, people eat anything they can get." At length the Giant invited Rabbit to a feast.

"Oh ho!" called the man whose lodge Rabbit had entered. "Friend, you are invited. Hasten!" Now all the people were afraid of Giant. No matter what animal anyone killed, the Giant kept all of the meat.

Rabbit arrived at the lodge of the Giant. As he entered, the host said, "Oh! Pass around to that side." But Rabbit leaped over and took a seat. At length food was given him. He ate it very rapidly but left some, which he hid in his robe. Then he pushed the bowl aside.

"Friend," he said to the Giant, "here is the bowl." Then he said, "Friend, I must go." He sprang past the fireplace at one leap, at the second leap his feet touched the chest of the Giant's servant, and with another leap he had gone.

When Rabbit reached the lodge where he was visiting, he gave his host the food he had not eaten. The man and his wife were glad to eat it, since they had been without food.

Next morning, the crier passed through the village, commanding the people to be stirring. They said, "The Giant is the one for whom they are to kill game." So they all went hunting. They scared some animals out of a dense forest and shot at them. Rabbit went thither very quickly. He found Giant had reached there before him and taken all the game. When Rabbit heard shooting in another place, he went thither, but again found the Giant was before him.

"This is provoking!" thought Rabbit. When some persons shot at game in another place Rabbit noticed it, and went thither immediately, reaching the spot before the Giant.

"Friend," he said to the man who had killed the deer, "let us cut it up." The man was unwilling. He said, "No, friend, the Giant will come by and by."

"Pshaw, friend," said Rabbit. "When one kills animals, he cuts them up and then makes an equal distribution of the pieces," said the Rabbit. Still the man refused, fearing the Giant. So Rabbit rushed forward and seized the deer by the feet. When he had only slit the skin, the Giant arrived.

"You have done wrong. Let it alone," Giant said.

"What have I done wrong?" asked Rabbit. "When one kills game, he cuts it up and makes an equal distribution of the pieces."

"Let it alone, I say," said the Giant. But the Rabbit continued to insert the knife in the meat. "I will blow that thing into the air," said the Giant.

"Blow me into the air! Blow me into the air!" said Rabbit.

So the Giant went closer to him, and when he blew at him the Rabbit went up into the air with his fur blown apart. Striding past, the Giant seized the deer, put it through his belt, and departed. That was his custom. He took all the deer that were killed, hung them on his belt, and took them to his lodge. He was a very tall person.

At night Rabbit wandered around, and at last went all around the Giant's lodge. He seized an insect and said to it, "Oh, insect! You shall go and bite the Giant right in the side."

At length when it was morning, it was said the Giant was ill. Then he died. The people said, "Make a village for Rabbit!"

But Rabbit said, "I do not wish to be chief. I have left my old woman by herself, so I will return to her."

continued ▶

Omaha myth continued...

This legend teaches many lessons. Do not be greedy like the giant, but rather share like the Rabbit. Fight back against oppressors. Working together is the best for everyone. At the end be humble in accepting praise. These are all important social lessons this legend passes on to others. By selecting the Rabbit to be the main character, the Omaha are emphasizing the importance of rabbit in their universal understanding. In general, rabbits must be of some significance to warrant being the hero of this story.

To the east and west, bluffs stand as boundaries to the American Bottom. These sandstone and limestone bluffs rise 30 to 60 meters (125-200 feet) above the floodplain. The Mississippi River hugs the western bluffs as it flows through the American Bottom. Occasional streams cut through the bluffs in narrow V-shaped channels. As these streams reach the bottom of the bluffs they spread out and deposit any sediment carried by the current. These deposits are known as alluvial fans, as they form a cone or fan shape when viewed from above. Fans are usually well drained and form an important link from the floodplain surface to the uplands. For Cahokians, alluvial fans were also a prime location for growing crops. The soil was fertile and well

The cone shaped alluvial fan is formed from sediment deposits built up by streams. The narrowest point is called the apex and the outer edge is referred to as the apron.

Section of the exhibit mural that depicts the bluffs bordering the American Bottom. These limestone or loess covered bluffs vary in height from 125-200 feet depending on their location.

drained, creating an optimal location for intensive agriculture.

Just bordering the bluffs running alongside the American Bottom are mosaics of prairie and deciduous forests. Strips of Illinois hill prairies stand along the southern and western facing bluffs. These steep prairies were dotted with thick and tall standing forests. To the northeast, groves of woods began to fade into sweeping tallgrass prairies in the uplands.

The environment's abundance of resources did not end at the floodplain's limits. The surrounding uplands were rich with diverse animals, plants, and minerals that were essential to Cahokia's survival and trade economy.

White-Tailed Deer

White-tailed deer were particularly important to Cahokia. Deer were the most frequently hunted mammal as they provided a substantial amount of meat per animal. While there is evidence of extensive consumption of waterfowl and fish, mammals, like white-tailed deer, added to the protein requirements of Cahokia's growing population. Deer were not just hunted for their meat. Other parts of the animals were also utilized by Cahokians. Bones, hides, antlers, hooves, sinews, and internal organs were all used in the creation of tools, shelter, clothing, cordage, glue and hide-tanning materials.

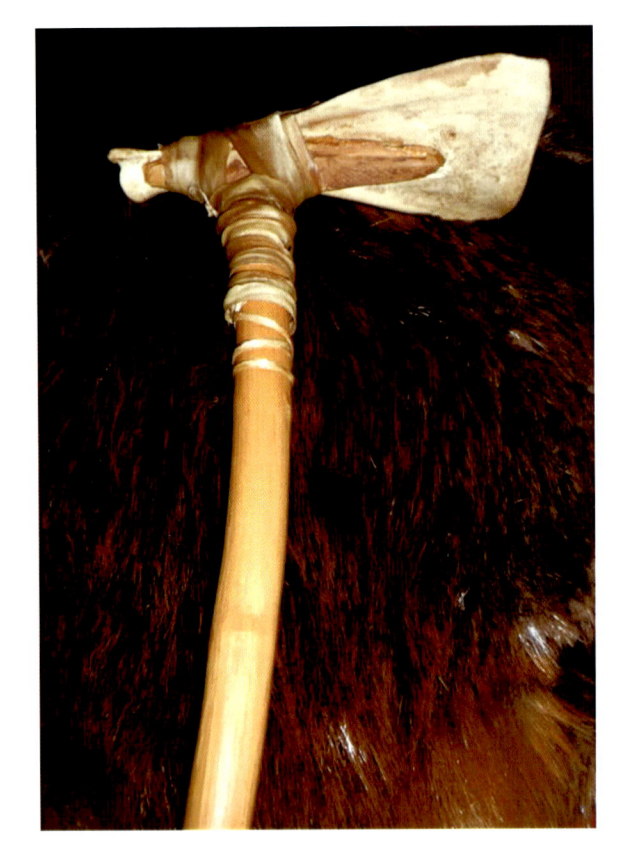

Photo of a white-tailed deer scapula hoe. Image courtesy of National Museum of the American Indian.

Photo of white-tailed deer on the site. Cahokians used all parts of the animal, for food, clothing, and tools. Image courtesy of Tom Miller.

There are many elements of the American Bottom that make it attractive to deer. The area is abundant in their preferred foods: tender shoots, twigs, leaves, certain fruits, and acorns. They especially love acorns, and there is a noticeable shift in their dietary attention in the fall to the newly dropped acorns. These also provide a food source during the winter months when shoots and leaves disappear. This illustrates another intricate relationship between Cahokia and the environment. For example, if Cahokians needed a significant amount of timber and cut down a large number of oaks, this would result in fewer acorns for the deer during the winter, which could impact the population.

As the human population boomed, deer populations would have moved farther away from the bustling urban center. This meant that the hunters would have had to travel farther to successfully hunt deer in order to supply their growing numbers. In the archaeological record we see a greater percentage of high utility (meatiest) parts of deer, which include the hind limbs and fore limbs. Perhaps hunters, finding themselves at increasingly greater distances from home, processed deer at the kill site in order to conserve energy and bring back the meatiest and most important portions of the kill.

Hunting deer throughout Cahokia's surrounding area would have taken more time and energy than catching fish in a local backwater lake. These hunts would have most likely taken place in late fall and winter months, when Cahokians had fewer demands on their time. Some suggest that there might have been a short summer hunt, but this would have only occurred while crops were growing and before harvest time. The ebbs and flows of hunting were intricately tied to seasonal resource availability. This system of seasonal exploitation was optimized to maximize yields, reduce adversity, and ensure survival.

The resources available to Cahokians in the American Bottom and surrounding lands far exceed what is described here. Every nook and cranny of wetland, forest, and prairie was home to some species of plant or animal. The Cahokians were a people who used their environment to the fullest, finding food, shelter, tools, and clothing- all of life's necessities from the world around them. They lived in a reciprocal relationship, taking yet also giving to the world around them. The archaeological objects and traditional stories that survive today are evidence of how Cahokians and other Mississippians valued their environment.

Aerial view of the Grand Plaza with Monks Mound to the north and the Twin Mounds at the south. Photo Courtesy, Matt Gush

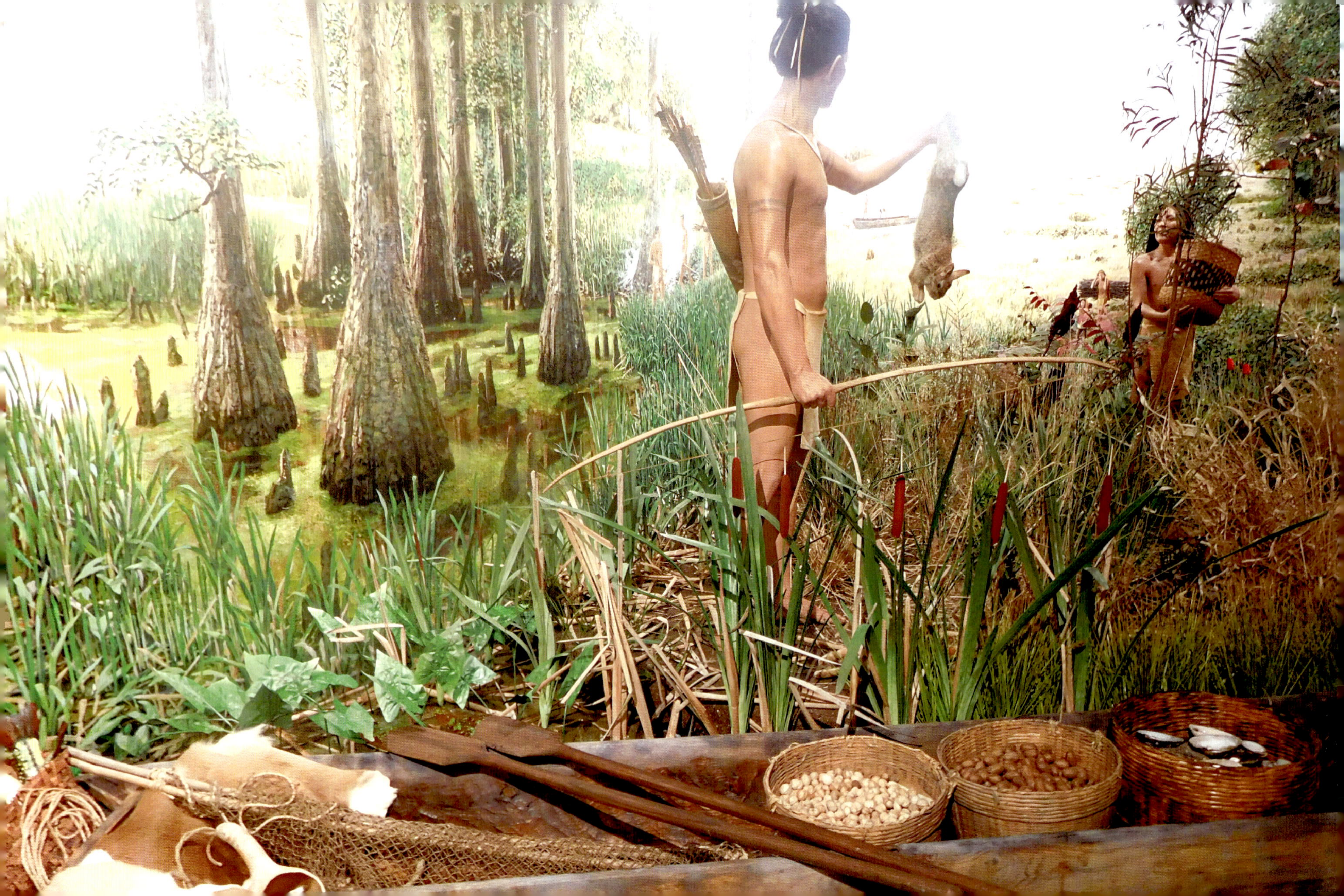

EXHIBIT *Wetlands And Waterways:*
The Key To Cahokia

Discussions about the potential exhibition featuring the newly-acquired canoe began as early as 2009 but due to staffing and state budget constraints, these discussions were put on hold. It wasn't until the conservation neared completion, and the museum acquired a two-year Graduate Research Assistant that the opportunity was reexamined. The desire for a wetlands and waterways exhibit had been present in the minds of staff, volunteers, and supporters for quite some time. The newly-acquired canoe and an in-depth interpretation of its role in Mississippian tradition was sure to pique the interest of potential visitors, supporters, and the media as well, and would be a significant compliment to the story of the Cahokians already presented in the museum. All of these factors led to the decision to develop this content-rich exhibit, thereby filling the objectives of the site, the intern, and most importantly, the community. A stakeholder committee was organized in 2013 consisting of Molly Wawrzyniak, site Graduate Research Assistant and Project Coordinator; Mark Esarey, Ph.D. Site Superintendent; Bill Iseminger, Site Assistant Manager; Lori Belknap, Executive Director of the Cahokia Mounds Museum Society (CMMS), the support group at the State Historic Site; with content-expert advisors, Gayle Fritz Ph.D., Professor, Washington University – St. Louis; Matt Migalla, Site Assistant Manager; Joe Seago, Site Technician; and Gene Stratmann, Site Technician.

Requests for proposals were sent out by CMMS to several highly-acclaimed design teams to produce an exhibit in the Interpretive Center gallery, centered on the ancient dugout. After receiving proposals from several well-qualified exhibit design teams, CMMS entered into an agreement with Riccio Exhibit Services (RES), Lerna, IL. RES has designed and fabricated various interpretive exhibits, including a permanent exhibit at the site titled, *Cahokia's Ancient Sun Calendar*, which was completed in 2010. RES has produced the two exhibits, *Rediscovering Tyrannosaurus-rex* and *René-Robert Cavelier, Sieur de La Salle Expedition Diorama* at Elgin Public Museum, Elgin, IL.

RES' concept was a descriptive approach with a life-sized diorama as a main display technique. The left side of the diorama depicting the bluffs, prairie and cultivated fields and the resources found in those ecozone. As the visitor moves through the 52-foot diorama, the wetland environment is depicted, with the canoe as the centerpiece of this segment. The center would also feature an aquatic segment in the floor, with an acrylic top, designed to look like the edge of a body of water. This would allow the viewer to see what types of resources were available beneath the surface, as well as in the shallow marshes along the shore. To the right,

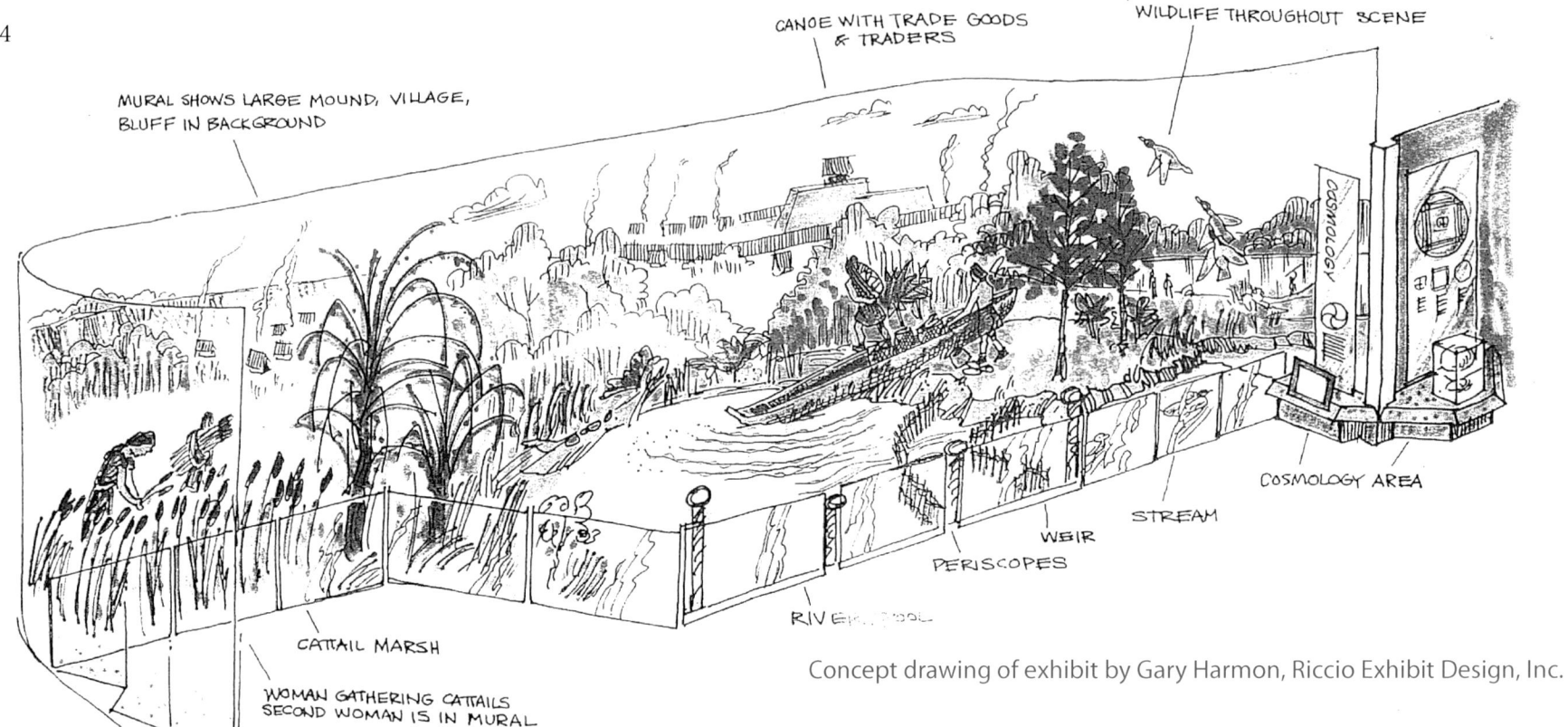

Concept drawing of exhibit by Gary Harmon, Riccio Exhibit Design, Inc.

would be the bottomland forest depiction. Interpretations in this area would focus on the plants and animals that Cahokians exploited in the low lying forest environment.

A Design Brief, which would serve as a template for the goals and objectives for the design phase, was circulated to the committee for completion. The Design Brief included questions that prompted the committee to develop the "big idea" and what details were to be communicated to the visitor. It included questions like: What are the take-home messages of the exhibit? What is the "big idea?" What is the "point of view?" What are the educational goals of the exhibit? What are the design opportunities and constraints? Before addressing the design questions, a visitor survey was conducted in the lobby to gain a better understanding of our visitor's expectations for the exhibit as well as their existing knowledge of the topic. By the end of this phase, a Design Brief was developed and agreed on by the site staff, the design team, and CMMS.

The exhibit would include a mural on the back wall that spanned the entirety of the diorama and gave the viewer a general understanding of the various ecozones in the American Bottom. While this would be a condensed version of the landscape, the committee felt it was necessary for the viewer's understanding of the resources that were available to the Cahokians.

After receiving several proposals, from some very talented muralists, the committee agreed on Jan Vriesen of Vriesen and Vriesen Studios, Milaca, MN.

The concept of the mural was to depict a scene from late summer/early fall during the height of Cahokia's prominence. The scene would depict three major environmental zones that exist in the

Concept model of exhibit by Gary Harmon, Riccio Exhibit Design, Inc.

Jan Vriesen making modifications to the installed mural.

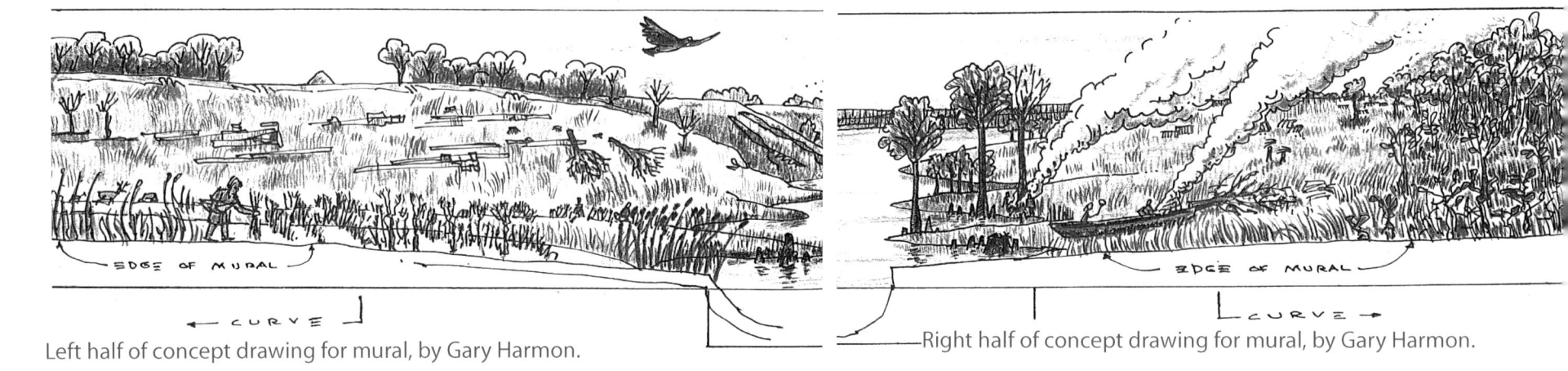

Left half of concept drawing for mural, by Gary Harmon.

Right half of concept drawing for mural, by Gary Harmon.

American Bottom, namely, wetlands, bottomland forest, and prairie. All plants and animals were to be painted realistically enough to identify species and Native Americans were to be depicted authentically, to the best of our understanding. The scene was to take place several miles from the center of Cahokia, so no major mounds or site features will be visible. Great depth of field was required and would be achieved by depicting elements of differing scale and the gradual loss of detail as the scene fades into the background. The bluffs that bank the east side of the American Bottom floodplain would be visible, as well as the bottomland forest.

During the planning phase, it quickly became apparent that the ancient canoe was too long to feature in the diorama without severely handicapping the perspective of the mural. At this juncture, it was determined that a separate exhibit case would be necessary to house the canoe, independent of the exhibit, and that a different canoe would have to be acquired for the diorama. It was decided to place the canoe case along the entrance ramp to the gallery, along the east side. The search began for a suitable canoe to serve as the centerpiece of the waterway section of the diorama. The ancient canoe was to be the pinnacle of the interpretation, so its departure from the exhibit made a significant impact on the planning.

Luckily, Gene Stratmann had fabricated a dugout canoe, about eight years previous, for use at Lewis and Clark State Historic Site as part of their interpretive gallery. That canoe was 12 feet 10 inches long, and although still a bit longer than ideal, it was the best option. Dr. Esarey spoke with the Superintendent at Lewis and

Clark, Brad Winn, and arranged to obtain it in trade for a different replica that Mr. Stratmann made.

The implementation phase involved the fabrication of the various components. A construction wall was installed in June at the exhibit perimeter to protect the visitors and the fabrication team, as well as obscure the exhibit from view. The next six months involved a flurry of design and planning activities as well as the compilation of research and materials.

During this stage, label copy was planned, mock-ups made, and content edited by the committee. Molly worked closely with Paleoethnobotanist, Gayle Fritz Ph.D., to compile appropriate descriptions of the floral resources, and consulted Lucretia Kelly Ph.D., regarding faunal descriptions, which would be incorporated in the mural. The design team worked closely with the committee regarding such things as, various ways to best depict the cosmol-

Labels: What's the "Big Idea"

LABELS (TEXT PANELS OR OTHER SIGNAGE) ARE AN IMPORTANT COMPONENT OF any exhibition and come in a variety of formats. Even though recent studies show that museum visitors read less than 50% of the labels, they still expect them as part of their interpretive experience. Labels are a necessary component of most exhibits and convey a variety of information to the viewer, ranging from specific details to general understanding, while always linking back to the "big idea" of your exhibit. The big idea is a statement of what the exhibition is about, but often there are secondary and tertiary messages that the team wishes to convey to the visitor.

While specific guidelines vary based on the institution and the exhibit, there are a few general guidelines that ensure the exhibit is as accessible as possible. There is no universal format when it comes to label writing. Each institution and exhibit is unique and tells a unique story to the viewer. Depending on the audience, the organization, and individual elements of the exhibit, the combination of objects, and displays, labels will vary from exhibit to exhibit. Regardless of the factors involved, they should be able to function independently, possessing internal integrity, yet still reflect back to the system as a whole. Following well-researched guidelines when writing and producing labels will help to guide traffic flow, make clear to viewers whose voice is represented with the exhibit, and ensure that the "big idea" is conveyed to as many as possible.

ogy of the Cahokians, what types of fowl should be displayed over the diorama, what collection of animals should be represented, how many mannequins there should be, and what ages and genders should the mannequins represent. A mockup of the placement of the animals in the water was done using cardboard shapes.

Cosmology, loosely defined here as a belief system that elucidates the order of the universe and an individual's place in it, is a difficult concept to communicate to visitors via an exhibit. This content may be the first exposure to concepts like world views, belief systems of Native Americans, or iconography, the tangible manifestation of these beliefs. Care must be taken to properly describe what we interpret as the cosmological model of the Cahokians, without interjecting our own contemporary views. Since there are no written records from the Cahokians, and so little is understood about their culture, it's difficult to say definitively what the ancient people's worldview was. There are over 100 contemporary Native American groups that have varying degrees of lineage to the ancient people of the eastern woodlands. One of these groups is the Osage. The decision was made to feature the Osage worldview in the cosmology video as an example of a cosmological model. There are many commonalities between iconography in the Osage traditions and what we find in the Mississippian culture, making this example a logical option. Specifically, depictions of birdman, underwater panther, and center poles are noted in the Osage model and images of these are depicted on Mississippian materials recovered at Cahokia and other Mississippian centers. Designing this component of the exhibit was a delicate endeavor and required careful thought and advice. James R. Duncan, who is of Osage descent, served as a Native American content advisor for the exhibit, and was instrumental in developing this feature.

Plant and animal place markers for water segment of exhibit.

A section of the exhibit was designed to include a video explaining the three worlds of the Osage worldview. It would especially focus on the importance of water and those animals that travel between the three spiritual realms (lower world, middle world, and underworld), and would be accompanied by an exhibit case displaying artifacts and artifact reproductions that depict iconography associated with this model. RES contracted with Heroic Age Studio to produce the cosmology video.

It was recommended by James Duncan that the video producers interview Osage Holy man, Charles Pratt, regarding this topic. At his request, a trip was arranged in November to travel to Oklahoma to interview Charles. The video features James' and Charles' alternating explanations of the cosmological model and associated iconography. This eight-minute video feature is a dynamic way to present these complex concepts to the visitor.

Mr. Vriesen painted the mural scene in his Minnesota studio on three 34 inch x 64 inch Masonite panels, producing the image at one-quarter scale. The panels would be digitally enlarged and printed onto a wallpaper-like medium and mounted to the wall. By doing so, this preserved the original painting in the event something happens to the building or the exhibit. When the painting was delivered, it was taken to Allied Photocolor Imaging Lab., St. Louis, MO, to be enlarged and printed to the vinyl medium that was fixed to the wall, by Leach Painting Company. After this step, Mr. Vriesen came to the site for 10 days to touch-up the mural directly on the wall. Many of the details that were present on the one-quarter-scale painting were lost in the enlarged version, particularly in the depicted people. In addition, some of

Leach Painting Company installing the mural.

the colors did not translate well, and the immediate foreground had some scale and color issues matching the background of the diorama. He worked diligently to mitigate these issues by touching up the artwork directly on the wall surface and the resulting product was a marked improvement over the original.

The diorama fabrication process was the most labor-intensive part of the exhibit production. Countless hours were spent by the design team acquiring the multitude of materials needed. The first stage was to install any wiring that was needed, whether it electric or speaker wire. This was followed by the plywood base, which was topped with a sculpted unit consisting of thick Styrofoam with a layer of fiberglass affixed to it. After the landscape base was in place, the design team fabricated a mixture of wood glue, sawdust, sand, garden soil, and paint. This was applied to the entire surface of the diorama to simulate the soil.

After the base was in place the fabrication duties continued and ranged from installing taxidermy items, skins, mussel shells, and baskets to be used in the canoe, and various plants that could either be used directly in the diorama or used to produce casting. The canoe had to be affixed and all of the animals mounted. Molding and casting the plethora of plants, cultivated crops, and trees was a time-consuming task. Clear acrylic pieces were mounted in the diorama middle section to simulate a water surface, with wet-

Rick Riccio, Riccio Exhibit Design, Inc., fabricating the diorama base.

Graduate Assistant, Molly working on exhibit base.

Molding and Casting

Molding and casting objects is a way to insert realistic objects into a display. Casts are reproductions of objects, made by pouring a material, such as a plaster or resin, into a mold. This process is most easily done on objects that are less-porous. A mold box is first manufactured to contain the item to be casted. Depending on the size of the item, this could be a cardboard box or a large, constructed, wooden frame. For our purpose, the design team used a vulcanizing rubber material. This is poured into the mold, it cures overnight, and the next day the mold can be removed in two halves. To produce the cast, the mold halves are adjoined and held together with bands. An epoxy resin is poured into the mold and allowed to cure. Once cured, the mold can be taken apart and the cast can then be cleaned of any seams and painted or finished in some other way. While the materials are not inexpensive, and the process can be time consuming, this is a very popular and efficient way to reproduce objects for a variety of uses, including plants, artifacts, and other materials.

Molding box for use in molding and casting process for diorama.

Cast mussels for use in the diorama.

Gary Harmon pouring the rubber material into the molding box.

land plants strategically placed around the edges so it had a realistic depiction of the canoe being pulled out of the water edge and onto the land surface. Any of the natural grasses that were added to the diorama were treated using an insecticide, a fire retardant, and sprayed with watered-down glue to make them a bit stiffer so they maintain their shape for a longer period.

Meanwhile, Taylor Studios, Inc., Rantoul, Illinois, fabricated the mannequins that would be used in the diorama. Three mannequins would be produced to communicate various roles people played in this particular environment. A pre-teen boy carries a basket and looks at a nearby adult male, who is loading the canoe with some game and other resources in baskets. A woman is kneeling in the garden section, she is cultivating squash and looking over at the two males. Some of the decisions that needed to be made by the committee were: what shade of skin should be used? What hairstyles? What facial expressions, and what types of clothing appropriate for the season and the time period? Should we add tattoos or other adornments? What was the best way to accurately depict our interpretations of Cahokians? Even selecting the appropriate body style and finding a suitable model was an arduous task.

The journey of the ancient canoe to its final home in the exhibit case was yet another challenge. The restoration took place inside of the site maintenance building, a large garage where

Installing the canoe exhibit, using gantry crane.

heavy equipment is stored and maintained. As summer approached, the canoe, which had been drying, began to leach out some of the PEG and it became apparent that the erratic environment of the garage wasn't the best suited location for the canoe to dry out and be ready for display. In June 2015, the canoe had to be moved to a private bay in the building that had a bit more of a controlled environment. This involved constructing two "wagons" mounted to casters. The canoe was then pulled off its stand with a tractor and onto the two-wagon cart. It was then wheeled over to its temporary holding bay, where it could continue to dry out. The canoe exhibit case was installed inside the gallery in the interim and on June 22, the canoe was rolled across Collinsville Rd., down Ramey St., and into the museum. A gantry crane was installed over the exhibit case. The crane was used to lift the canoe off the cart, and lower it onto its support inside the exhibit case, where it will remain on display.

The last items to be installed in the exhibit were the artifacts and artifact replications. The final stage of the fabrication process was a walk-through to identify any potential issues that needed to be corrected. Hair styles were manicured, construction and mounting materials were removed or hidden, and bare spots in the landscape were filled. A maintenance plan and warranty listing was provided by the designers at the close of the exhibit production. The exhibit was complete and, after two years, a grand unveiling in mid-August brought two important aspects of Mississippian culture to the public- an extensive exhibit depicting the interconnectedness of life in the American Bottom, and an artifact that serves as an exemplar of Native American ingenuity and craftsmanship.

Moving the canoe into the Interpretive Center.

CONCLUSION

This book serves as an accompaniment to the recent discovery and display of the ancient canoe and new exhibit *Wetlands and Waterways: The Key to Cahokia*. While there is much we don't know about the Cahokians, new research continues to expand our knowledge of the beginnings of Cahokia and this unique city they created, its long occupation of the region, and its eventual decline. What specific factors led to the Cahokia's florescence and demise are probably myriad. As more research is conducted, our understanding of the events will expand. However, the use of the canoe as a mode of transportation and travel, and its associated role as a cultural transmitter, was vital to the success of the city. The unique landscape feature of connected waterways, the extensive floodplain environment and the abundance and variety of wetland resources found in its ecosystems, coupled with the use of the dugout canoe, is the key to the city's growth and prosperity.

THE CAHOKIA MOUNDS MUSEUM SOCIETY (CMMS) is the not-for-profit support group for Cahokia Mounds State Historic Site. CMMS is committed to ongoing preservation, restoration, research, and interpretation at Cahokia and to continued expansion of the protected area. Join CMMS to receive your quarterly newsletter with the latest information about activities, events, and new research at the site. Your membership supports land acquisition, research, and public outreach and educational events at Cahokia Mounds.

Cahokia Mounds Museum Society
30 Ramey Street
Collinsville, IL 62234
(618)344-7316
www.cahokiamounds.org

Cahokia Mounds State Historic Site
30 Ramey Street
Collinsville, IL 62234
(618)346-5160
www.cahokiamounds.org

MISSION STATEMENTS

Cahokia Mounds Museum Society Mission Statement:
The purpose of the Society shall be to promote for the public benefit the educational and scientific aspects of the Cahokia Mounds Historic Site and associated archaeological sphere. For the better fulfillment of these purposes, the Society will seek to cooperate with the Illinois Historic Preservation Agency (or its successor) and with other state, federal and local agencies, institutions, or organizations, both public and private, having common interests. To attain its objectives, the Society may assist in developing and maintaining a museum or interpretive center, promote research, publish scientific and popular reports, hold meetings and sponsor lectures, promote educational programs and projects, and otherwise engage in any activity that is calculated to conserve, develop or interpret the Cahokia Mounds Historic Site and its related archaeological sphere.

Cahokia Mounds State Historic Site Mission Statement:
The primary objective of the State Historic Site is to preserve, restore, and interpret the cultural development of the site for the mutual benefit of the citizens of Illinois and the World. Secondary objectives include the protection and enhancement of natural heritage and significant wildlife areas within the site to illustrate the inter-relationships that existed between the site's prehistoric inhabitants and their environment, provision of service facilities, and provision of limited day-use support facilities.

BIBLIOGRAPHY

Brown, James A. "The Cahokian Expression: Creating Court and Cult." In *Hero, Hawk, and Open Hand: American Indian Art of the Ancient Midwest and South*, edited by Richard F. Townsend, 105-124. Chicago: The Art Institute of Chicago, 2004.

Brown, James A, Richards A. Kerber, and Howard D. Winter. "Trade and the Evolution of Exchange Relations at the Beginning of the Mississippian Period." In *The Mississippian Emergence*, edited by Bruce D. Smith, 251-274. Washington: Smithsonian Institution Press, 1990.

Chomko, Stephen A. and Gary W. Crawford. "Plant Husbandry in Prehistoric Eastern North America: New Evidence for its Development." In *American Antiquity* 43, No. 3 (1978): 405-408.

Fontana, Marisa D. *Of Walls and War: Fortification and Warfare in the Mississippian Southeast*, Thesis submitted for Doctor of Philosophy in Anthropology. University of Illinois at Chicago. Chicago, Illinois. 2007.

Fritz, G.J. and N. H. Lopinot. "Native Crops at Early Cahokia: Comparing Domestic and Ceremonial Contexts." In *People, Plants, and Animals: Archaeological Studies of Human-Environment Interactions in the Midcontinent, Essays in Honor of Leonard W. Blake*, edited by R. E. Warren. *Illinois Archaeology* 15 & 16 (2007):90-111.

Fritz, G.J. "Levels of biodiversity in eastern North America." In *Biodiversity and Native America*, edited by P. E. Minnis and W. Elisens, 223-247. University of Oklahoma Press: Norman, 2000.

Gardner, Paul S. "New Evidence Concerning the Chronology and Paleoethnobotany of Salts Cave, Kentucky." In *American Antiquity* 52, No. 2 (1987): 358-367.

Gregg, Michael Lee. "Settlement Morphology and Production Specialization: The Horseshoe Lake Site, A Case Study." Thesis submitted for Doctor of Philosophy in Anthropology, The University of Wisconsin-Milwaukee, 1975.

Goldberg, Paul and Richard I. Macphail. *Practical and Theoretical Geoarchaeology*. Oxford: Blackwell Publishing, 2006.

Hartmann, Mark Joseph. "The Development of Watercraft in the Prehistoric Southeastern United States." Thesis submitted for Doctor of Philosophy in Anthropology, Texas A&M University, 1996.

Hudson, Charles. "The Hernando DeSoto Expedition, 1539-1543." In Charles Hudson and Carmen C. Tesser *The Forgotten Centuries: Indians and Europeans in the American South, 1521-1704*, 74-203. The University of Georgia Press, Athens 1994.

Iseminger, William. *Cahokia Mounds: America's First City*. Charleston: The History Press, 2010.

Iseminger, William R. "Culture and Environment in the American Bottom: The Rise and Fall of Cahokia Mounds." In *Common Fields an Environmental History of St. Louis*, edited by Andrew Hurley, 38-57. Saint Louis: Missouri Historical Society Press, 1997.

Iseminger, William R. "Identifying and Understanding Artifacts of Illinois and Neighboring States." In *Illinois Association of Advancement of Archaeology*. Occasional Journal Vol. 6, 2014.

Johannessen, Sissel. "Paleoethnobotany." In *American Bottom Archaeology: A Summary of the FAI-270 Project Contribution to the Culture History of the Mississippi River Valley*, edited by Charles J. Bareis and James W. Porter, 197-214. Urbana: University of Illinois Press, 1984.

Judson, Katherine Berry (editor). *Myths and Legends of the Great Plains*. EBook #22083. July 16, 2007.

Kelly, John E., James A. Brown, Jenna M. Hamlin, Lucretia S. Kelly, Laura Kozuch, Kathryn Parker, and Julieann Van Nest, " Mound 34: The Context for the Early Evidence of the Southeastern Ceremonial Complex at Cahokia." In *Chronology, Iconography, and Style: Current Perspectives on the Social and Temporal Contexts of the Southeastern Ceremonial Complex,* edited by Adam King. Tuscaloosa: University of Alabama Press, 2007.

Kelly, Lucretia S. and Paula G. Cross. "Zooarchaeology." In *American Bottom Archaeology: A Summary of the FAI-270 Project Contribution to the Culture History of the Mississippi River Valley*, edited by Charles J. Bareis and James W. Porter, 215-232. Urbana: University of Illinois Press, 1984.

Kelly, Lucretia Starr Schryver. "Social Implications of Faunal Provisioning for the Cahokia Site: Initial Mississippian, Lohmann Phase." Thesis submitted for Doctor of Philosophy in Anthropology, Washington University in St. Louis, 2000.

Kuehn, Steven R. "Faunal Remains." In *The Archaeology of Downtown Cahokia II: The 1960 Excavation of Tract 15B*, edited by Timothy R. Pauketat, 275-298. Urbana: University of Illinois Press, 2013.

Lankford, George E. "World on a String: Some Cosmological Components of the Southeastern Ceremonial Complex." In *Hero, Hawk, and Open Hand: American Indian Art of the Ancient Midwest and South*, edited by Richard F. Townsend, 207-218. Chicago: The Art Institute of Chicago, 2004.

Lankford, G.E., Kent F. Reilly III, and J.F. Garber, editors. *Visualizing the Sacred: Cosmic Visions, Regionalism, and the Art of the Mississippian World*. University of Texas Press, Austin. 2007.

Leader, Jonathan Max. "Technological Continuities and Specialization in Prehistoric Metalwork in the Eastern United States." Ph.D. dissertation, Department of Anthropology, University of Florida (1988).

Meide, Chuck. "The Dugout Canoe in the Americas: An Archaeological, Ethnohistorical, and Structural Overview." Paper submitted at Florida State University, 1995.

Milner, George R. *The Cahokian Chiefdom: The Archaeology of a Mississippian Society*. Washington: Smithsonian Institution Press, 1998.

Pauketat, Timothy R. *Ancient Cahokia and the Mississippians*. Cambridge: Cambridge University Press, 2004.

Phillips, Philip and James A. Brown. *Pre-Columbian Shell Engravings From the Craig Mound at Spiro, Oklahoma*. Cambridge: Peabody Museum Press, 1984.

Purdy, Barbara A. *The Art and Archaeology of Florida's Wetlands*. Boca Raton: CRC Press Inc., 1991.

Reilly, F. Kent III. "People of Earth, People of Sky: Visualizing the Sacred in Native American Art of the Mississippian Period." In *Hero, Hawk, and Open Hand: American Indian Art of the Ancient Midwest and South*, edited by Richard F. Townsend, 125-138. Chicago: The Art Institute of Chicago, 2004.

Salas, Catalina. "Retrodicting Climatic Sequences: Examining Relationships Between Climate and Populations in the Rise and Decline of Mississippian Culture Focusing on Cahokia." Honors Thesis, Hamline University, 1994.

Sampson, Kelvin and Duane Esarey. "A Survey of Elaborate Mississippian Copper Artifacts from Illinois." In *Journal of the Illinois Archaeological Survey* 5 (1 and 2): 452-474, 1993.

Schroeder, Walter. "The Environmental Setting of the St. Louis Region." In *Common Fields an Environmental History of St. Louis*, edited by Andrew Hurley, 13-37. Saint Louis: Missouri Historical Society Press, 1997.

White, William P., Sissel Johannessen, Paula G. Cross, and Lucretia S. Kelly. "Environmental Setting." In *American Bottom Archaeology: A Summary of the FAI-270 Project Contribution to the Culture History of the Mississippi River Valley*, edited by Charles J. Bareis and James W. Porter, 15-33. Urbana: University of Illinois Press, 1984.

Wilson, Gilbert Livingston. *Agriculture of the Hidatsa Indians, An Indian Interpretation*. Reprints in Anthropology, Vol. 5. Lincoln, Nebraska: J&L Reprint Company, 1977. Referenced as, Buffalo Bird Woman's Garden in text.

Yerkes, Richard W. "Microwear, Microdrills, and Mississippian Craft Specialization." In *American Antiquity* 48, no. 3 (July 1983): 499-518.